TOO SOON TO SAY "GOODBYE"

Review by Roland A. Frauchiger, M.A., MFT

This is both a remarkably warm and personal account of the emotional and behavioral consequences children and young adults suffer when the tragic loss of a parent occurs "too soon." A very easy read, and an engaging and informative treatment of the topic of parental loss from a professional psychotherapist, who has the courage to tell her own story of the loss of her father.

Combining research with a myriad of case histories, Phyllis Cohen Deitch, with great sensibility, sorts out and organizes the complex and often agonizing problems a family faces when the premature loss of a parent occurs. Whether the loss is of a mother or a father, or both, or occurs to a son or daughter, the effects on the values of trust, autonomy, ambition, creativity, and the expanding capacity for intimacy and love are seriously impacted. The shock and trauma of parental loss, which all too often results in the arrest of emotional learning, and educational and social development, can last a lifetime. Deitch notes, if not addressed, treated, and/or healed, these traumas including physical illness, can be passed on from generation to generation.

The author's narrative includes her own devastating loss of her father as a teenager, who was 55 when he passed. She describes the challenges her family struggled with in order to survive, and the stages of emotional and behavioral healing she had to work through to become the person she is today. This personal account is one of the strengths of this book. It is not a cold, academic work, or what one often encounters by professional authorities on mental health topics: a dry pedantic prescription in "how to." The reader who is seeking guidance with his or her parental loss is reassured through the example of courage set by the author's own discloser in writing the story of her own loss and recovery.

In Chapter 7, Creative Outcomes, the author addressed the adaptive healing power of the mind/body to overcome personal adversity by stimulating and reinforcing abilities and talents that may not have been actualized except for the necessity to survive. There are many familiar examples of this kind of mind/body response during war and disasters, when extraordinary actions of courage and creativity are brought out in individuals. This book mentions many famous people who lost a parent as a child, adolescent, or young adult and includes some of their interesting stories and quotes.

Phyllis Cohen Deitch's book, "Too Soon to Say 'Goodbye'," stays true to her intention: to share her story of loss in the hope it will help others who have experienced parental loss to become aware and to find healing by sharing their own stories.

Printed in the United States of America

Published by Eifrig Publishing, LLC
PO Box 66, 701 Berry Street, Lemont, PA 16851.
Knobelsdorffstr. 44, 14059 Berlin, Germany

For information regarding permission, write to:
Rights and Permissions Department,
Eifrig Publishing, LLC
PO Box 66, 701 Berry Street, Lemont, PA 16851, USA.
permissions@eifrigpublishing.com, 888-340-6543.

Library of Congress Cataloging-in-Publication Data

Deitch, Phyllis Cohen
Too Soon to Say "Goodbye" / written by Phyllis Cohen Deitch
    p.   cm.

Paperback: ISBN 978-1-936172-60-3

1. PSYCHOLOGY: Death, Loss, Parent Loss, Recovery from Loss

I. Deitch, Phyllis Cohen II. Title.

17 16 15 14 2013
5 4 3 2 1

Printed on acid-free paper. ∞

TOO SOON TO SAY "GOODBYE"

When You Have Lost a Parent as a Child,
Adolescent, or Young Adult

To Terry & Marvin –
Long ago friends and now
family – How lucky we are to
share our precious children.
With warmest regards & love –
Phyllis

by

Phyllis Cohen Deitch

Eifrig Publishing LLC
Lemont   Berlin

Acknowledgments

My enormous appreciation and gratitude go out to the courageous people who kindly and willingly shared their personal stories with me. Without their interest and cooperation, this project could not have happened. Their input and contributions have been extremely valuable. I thank them all for their time, openness and generosity of spirit. Special thanks also to my wonderful family and friends who read many early drafts and provided valuable feedback.

I acknowledge with deepest gratitude and appreciation Dr. Salman Akhtar, Daniel Cohn, Margie Granach, and Lois Figlin, who have provided encouragement and support as this project grew from notes jotted on loose pieces of scrap paper through several drafts of a manuscript to its final completion. They have been most generous with their time, and provided me with friendship, inspiration, mentorship, wisdom, and knowledge from their particular areas of expertise. Most sincere thanks and gratitude also go to my dear husband, Dr. Bernard Deitch, who has never wavered in his support, encouragement and practical help whenever needed. Without his dedication, this project could not have continued. With much appreciation I acknowledge both Roland Frauchiger and Dr. Julius Romanoff, who each provided employment, encouraged my continued education, and facilitated the development of my professional growth. I thank them for their ability to enhance my knowledge and development of my skills, and for continuing to be available and interested in my work. My thanks also to my siblings, Robert and Susan Cohen, and Dr. Joshua and Lois Figlin. They have supported me from the beginning, and they continue to be an important part of my life. A heartfelt thank you goes out to Chris Penney, Debra Penney, and Jacqueline D. Scarborough. Their computer expertise, creative skills and untiring perseverance in meeting deadlines, have brought this project from handwritten pages to an elegant manuscript.

I feel so proud of my wonderful family. They have brought me so much pleasure and provided me with all the most meaningful aspects of my life. I continue to be inspired by them and I am sustained by their love, support, encouragement, wisdom and humor. My love and deepest gratitude go to my dear and precious family: my husband – Bernard Deitch; my children – Roger and Michele Cohn, Debra Penney and Allen Kelmer, Daniel and Stephanie Cohn; and my grandchildren – Chris, Kevin, Caitlin, Alexis, Sophia, and Jeremy. I treasure you all and thank you for your ability to provide me with joy and laughter.

Phyllis Deitch

CONTENTS

My Intention   7

Chapter 1 Is There a "Good" Time to Lose a Parent?   9
     My Story - Part I – Reflections

Chapter 2 Loss of Mother   15

     Part I: Daughters and Loss of Mother in Early Childhood –
Some Fears – Daughters and Loss of Mother through Adolescence
– Daughters and Loss of Mother in Teen Years – Daughters and
Loss of Mother in Early Adulthood – Reflections

     Part II: Sons and Loss of Mother in Childhood – Sons and Loss of
Mother in Teen Years – Reflections

Chapter 3 Loss of Father   31

     Part I: Daughters and Loss of Father – Daughters and Loss of
Father in Childhood – Daughters and Loss of Father in Teen Years –
My Story - Part II – Reflections

     Part II: Sons and Loss of Father – Sons and Loss of Father in
Childhood – Sons and Loss of Father in Teen Years – Reflections

Chapter 4 Loss of Both Parents   57
     Orphans – Reflections

Chapter 5 Going forward   67
     Anniversary Times – Visiting Graves – Reflections

Chapter 6 Impact of Parental Loss on the Next Generation   73
     Wounds – Worries – Reflections

Chapter 7 Creative Outcomes   81
     Famous People Who Lost a Parent as a Child, Adolescent or Young
Adult – Stories and Quotes from Famous People – Reflections

Chapter 8 Ways People Heal   91

     The Younger Child and Healing – The Teen and Healing –
The Young Adult and Healing – Reflections

References   113

With loving memory
in honor of my dear parents,
Betty and Irving Cohen

My Intention

As a psychotherapist working with adults over many years, I became aware of the repetition of the same pattern. People of all ages in the first few minutes of their therapy session would say: "I was 6/8/12/18 when my father/mother died." Then they would quickly add, "But that's not why I am here."

When asked to tell their story, I heard many of the same facts and feelings repeated. Their stories, reactions, and emotions seemed to be universal. I soon realized the effects of early parent loss run deep and have profound consequences. Early traumas continue to reside just beneath the surface and tend to become a mark of identification carried from that awful moment forward throughout life. Even those who believed they were no longer affected because the trauma happened so long ago still seemed burdened in some deep way. Since I, too, share this burden, I began to pay closer attention.

In order to learn more, I interviewed over 100 adults who sustained loss of one or both parents from 6 months through 26 years of age. I was searching for information and inspiration toward overcoming those early effects and bringing about healing. It is my hope that others can identify, find some comfort, gain understanding of their feelings, begin their personal journey toward healing, and be empowered to reach their true potential.

As a therapist and while exploring the effects of early parent loss, I saw how beneficial it was for people to tell their stories. I, then, began to write and learned how healing it was for me to tell my own story. This book is about my personal experiences as well as those of the many people who so bravely shared their stories with me. It is my hope that it will be read by those adults who have experienced early parent loss and for those whose lives have been touched by it. These include, but are not limited to, spouses, surviving parents and other caretakers, teachers, and therapists. It is my desire to increase awareness and understanding of early loss and to encourage healing.

Chapter 1

Is there a "good" time to lose a parent?

This is the year my mom would have been 101 and my dad 107 years old. This year, 2012, would have been a good time for them to leave us. For most of my life I have had this inner dialogue: "Okay, Mom, Okay, Dad, this would have been a good time" or I'd think "How about now... or now...or now" – any time other than when it happened would have been a better or more acceptable time. "It was too soon for you to go; it was not the right time for you to leave." I imagine at age 101 and 107 I'd feel satisfied and filled with gratitude.

Today, at 70, through so many of my own personal milestones and life experiences as a wife, mother, grandmother, sister, friend and therapist, I am deeply aware that the death of a parent when one is a child, adolescent or young adult is painful and always sad for those who are left. No matter when it happens, it's always too soon and it's never a good or right time.

And yet, when I see older adult children grieving the loss of their very elderly parents, I feel confused and amazed. I can only think "how lucky they all were to have had each other for so long." Instead of tears, I feel they should be thankful and rejoice for their gift of longevity. They should be celebrating their parents' presence at each milestone of their lives. I realize they don't even know how lucky they were to have the lifelong gift of a parent; they never knew any other reality. I cannot relate to their tears. All I can feel is envy.

I feel a lot of guilt having these feelings. I feel greedy for having wanted so much more for myself and my family. I feel ashamed that I lack the empathy I would normally have. As I look within and wonder about my emotions, which are so counterintuitive to me as a therapist, I realize that even today, after I've worked so hard in my personal healing and worked for so many years as a therapist helping others, deep within my heart of hearts, I still feel the pain of the anger – the same anger I believed I had come to terms with long ago. I now see that it never gets totally healed, never totally goes away, but continues to exist in a quieter place, ready to surface in moments of envy when I allow myself to think: "How much more time did these grieving adults want?" I guess they, like me, would have wanted lots more. As I see what remains in that quieter place, I am more able to allow myself the understanding and the empathy.

The loss of a parent is our fall from innocence. It is a realization that our lives will not necessarily progress as we had believed it would. It is hoped that one will achieve the tasks and skills needed at each developmental stage and there will be an easy transition from one stage to the next. One grows up believing life will unfold as we and our parents planned, and our future would be filled with the fulfillment of our dreams as well as theirs. We all share a certain innocence in our young lives, and believe all will continue to be as it is now, that we will be safe, loved, cared for, and that someday we will be the healthy adults in our best of all possible lives. With early parent loss, we go forward, but we are forever changed. We know that fate or life might have other plans for us. It is like taking the apple in the Garden of Eden, our paradise is gone. We now see and know the truth of life, and we can never go back to not knowing.

My Story – Part I

My dad has been gone for 53 years, almost as long as he had lived. He passed away when he was 55; the years of his life and the years since seem to have happened in the blink of an eye. Fifty-five is so very young; there is so much left to do, and so many people still depend on you for everyday life – for emotional support, security, guidance, love, etc.

Today, my own children are wonderful adults with marriages and children of their own. I see how quickly time passes. I have loved and enjoyed all of the days of their lives, and yet not a day goes by that I don't think about either my Dad or my Mom, who is gone now for 40 years. In an instant, just under the surface there is a memory or a feeling or a twinge of pain or a tear.

When my Dad died, he left three children. They were me, age 18, my brother, age 14, and my sister, age 8 1/2. When his own mother died, he was under two years of age and his brother was six months old, making me a member of the first generation of parent loss and also a second-generation member. He came from "the other side" as he would refer to his homeland of Russia. He was an observant Jew and came from the "Shtetl" to America at age 15, traveling with only his 13-year-old brother. It was 1920 and they lived in the lower east side of New York with the same aunts who cared for them as babies in Russia.

His belief was that a woman's role was wife and mother. Not much value was placed on education or careers for a woman. His greatest wish was for me to marry and have children. He looked forward to being a grandfather. When he became ill, I started a race to get married, even though I knew I was going to college because my Mom insisted. My focus was not on my studies; I could see nothing beyond my wedding day. I thought only of marriage to my boyfriend who was very loved by my parents. I knew I was racing against time. I had faith and prayed constantly. We both lost the race and our prayers were left unanswered.

His sadness and disappointment that he had to leave us so soon were sustained through me. His desires merged with my goals, and I could no longer distinguish his reality from mine. I felt a sense of urgency. I believed life is all too short, good people die young and prayers are not heard. I felt driven to marry, to have children of whom he would be so proud, and to be the best Mom possible. I needed to begin this life and live it quickly, before it was too late. The week I turned 20, I was married to my childhood sweetheart. I am not certain either of us was ready for marriage; we had not seriously dated others, and I'm sure we both lacked maturity. My heart was still broken and I was afraid to love too deeply. I already knew what can and does happen. I no longer prayed, my wedding day was planned with no real joy. I was saddened that my Dad was not there to walk me down the aisle, to stand by my side under the chuppah (the wedding canopy), to "kvell" (be thrilled) for me as only he knew how, to help make decisions or to furnish our first apartment since he was in the furniture business. I felt the absence of his smiling, sparkling eyes and his round, joyful face. I missed his voice saying, "Le Chaim" (to life) at the first toast. All this was too much to bear. I felt withdrawn inside myself and was only superficially present at my own wedding, at the only event I had ever looked forward to. I felt like a mannequin, all dressed up, playing the role of happy bride.

Our first child was born nine months later. While pregnant, I felt safe from all harm, all dangers. I knew I was meant to be a mother and nothing would happen to me or my baby. I felt blessed and certain my Dad's spirit and soul had become our guardian angel and that he was watching over us. When my son was born, I too felt a rebirth of life. I looked at his beautiful face and fell deeply in love with him. I felt he was a miracle and thought perhaps God does exist. I named him for my Dad and held onto him so tightly. I wanted always to keep him free from harm and free from the dangers of life. I bargained and I made deals – "I will be _____ I will do _____, but please God – please Daddy – keep us well and safe from harm." Later I learned how people who suffered early parent loss often merge God with the deceased parent, and at times, the two become interchangeable.

My husband and I lived a lovely life and had two more beautiful children, a daughter two years later and another son nine years later. I saw in my children various aspects of my Dad both physically and behaviorally. I yearned for my Dad and felt regret that he was not there to see and enjoy everything they said and did. I knew the unbridled pleasure he would have felt. He would have called our daughter "Debbelah" (a Yiddish affectionate name for Debbie) and he would have danced at his grandchildren's weddings and would have been thrilled by their delicious babies in whose faces I searched for traces of him. He has missed so much of the best of life.

My children, thankfully, have been successful, yet they and I have missed so very much by not having him in our lives. They lost the emotional richness of a loving, wise, good-hearted and generous man. Embodied in him was their religious and cultural heritage and of that they were regrettably deprived. My own sadness and missing of him was always most intense at holiday times and at all of our special milestones.

Reflections

As I have learned over many years as I work with my clients, we need to simultaneously prepare for what we want and plan to live a happy, fulfilling life while also being prepared for the unknown. The trick is to prevent the preparedness from advancing into anxiety or obsessive-compulsive disorder. The trick is to learn to carefully look but not become driven or hypervigilant. We learn that life does not always follow 1 – 2 – 3. We learn about what the ancient Jews referred to as "the Evil Eye."

There is also the acute sadness when a father is not present to walk his daughter down the aisle on her wedding day. At my wedding, my 40-year-old uncle had to stand in for my father. Then, two years later, he died, and 10 years later, he was not here to walk his own daughter down the aisle. The layers of emotion between my cousin and me have yet to be explored. Having our mothers stand alone under our chuppahs (wedding canopy), knowing their sadness and feelings of aloneness have added to our ongoing grief.

The great invader is the death of a parent, which occurs before the child is able to understand or cope well with this unexpected tragedy, which comes as a thief in the night and destroys life as we know it. Childhood loss can have lifelong impact. The child is attached to the parents and relies exclusively on them for sense of self and sense of security. Parents provide social maps of their world, interpreting and making sense of it for them. When a parent dies and loss comes so early, the child suffers a kind of death.

CHAPTER 2

Loss of Mother

It is not possible to grow up without loss. As the saying goes, "The fruit has to leave the tree." The task of the mother is to transfer her role to her children enabling them to have the capacity to be on their own successfully. It is mothers who are to be left and only after their children are safely grown and ready to be independent.

An important aspect is for a mother to be comfortable being a woman. This helps both the sons and daughters to develop. That is the way life is supposed to unfold. In early loss of mother, development is effected and growth is often stunted. From Mary Gordon's book, _The Rest of Life_, the character Paola says, "We were ignorant – with all our learning, poetry, history, philosophy and art, I had no mother. I was afraid to touch any part of my body that seemed secret. I didn't know what could be wrongly touched or damaged. I got my information from the air. I heard things in the air that nice people could not have said. I felt that girls with mothers knew things. I had no mother and knew nothing."

For most children, loss of their mother caused feelings of fury and rage. Their mantra was, "She left me, she promised she'd always be there for me, always come back home and she left me." These children had a deep loneliness and felt like an outsider, even with close friends and family. They felt they didn't belong and were isolated from social life. Many people described a deep sense of injustice – "life is unfair." Friends did not want to hear sad things, so they kept their feelings a secret. They felt no one would understand. They had a stigma and felt different from their peers.

Many said, "Since I don't have a mother, there is no one to love me." Since they felt no one would ever love them, they had a fear of intimacy, which often led to a self-fulfilling prophecy. When a child loses a mother and does not get mothered, the child feels unfulfilled and unappreciated. Even as an adult, one can continue to feel this deficit, which could lead to feeling defective, pessimistic, hopeless or depressed and often terrified of change.

Often, mourning was not encouraged. The surviving adults acted as if nothing happened. If mourning is bypassed, there is often depression and a lack of ability to form new attachments. The steps of mourning include anger, depression, acceptance of the loss, ability to form new attachments and a letting go. When a mother dies, often the father discourages the mourning process because he is too uncomfortable with his own grief. Some fathers have the attitude that the child should get on with life. He might even convince himself that the mother was not really missed. Sometimes, a father tells the child to keep memories private and keep all mementos in a box. There could even be requests to call a stepmother "Mom." Many complained that their father never spoke of their deceased mother. Often they were alienated physically or emotionally from their mother's family.

Some grew up having never learned to take good care of themselves emotionally or physically. Some experienced nightmares that repeated over many years. They fantasized or dreamed that their mother was away, living elsewhere and would someday return. They might fear that their mother is staying away as a punishment. They held onto the belief that their mother will be back and then everything will be okay. There is a denial and the concept of finality is difficult to grasp.

Part I
Daughters and Loss of Mother in Early Childhood

I met with many women whose responses to grief were delayed. They suffered loss of their mother in early childhood, yet the impact and grieving process did not begin until they were older and a particular life event became a trigger. Some talked about suffering from depression, crying often and being in emotional pain. As adults, these women were able to enter therapy and mourn for the first time. A woman who lost her mother when she was very young was finally able to get in touch with her mother's messages to "never give up" and "value every moment in life." She was able to hold onto these messages as she proceeded into adulthood and allowed them to strengthen her.

Patty, a young woman of 36 lost her 36-year-old mother when she was four years old. Raised by her father and stepmother, she felt alienated and abandoned because her caretakers paid very little attention to her and were not emotionally available. She grew up feeling lonely and scared. She developed the philosophy that good times can't last for too long. Patty believed that everything good will end and never be good again. She became a hypervigilant person, picking up all kinds of signals from people. Patty still tries to anticipate and avoid events that could potentially turn bad. She also worries when things go well and tells herself "this is not going to last."

Arriving at age 36, the same age her mother was when she died, Patty feared her own death this same year and she looked forward to getting beyond this year. She began to feel deprived. She had lacked a mother – a role model and motherly advice. She always longed for an adult-mother relationship. She realized that she tends to seek advice from women who are mother figures. Patty's beliefs are that she doesn't deserve good things, and that she will never marry. In her relationships, she feels she needs too much mothering. She tends to seek advice and lacks a strong sense of her own mind. Patty fears she is too dependent on others. Food calms her and drowns her pain, and she does tend to have a weight problem.

Some Fears

The young child is egocentric and relates everything to himself, believing he is the cause of all things. The child could see this major life change as something he did wrong. The youngest children at the time of the loss lack the cognitive ability to understand what happened.

Even older children can feel responsible for a mother's death. They often felt a lot of guilt and in order to cover these painful emotions, many developed phobias or obsessive-compulsive behaviors. Many rituals can dominate such as checking and double-checking in every task, hand washing, nail biting, addictive behaviors and overeating. Having anxiety attacks, fears of illness and fears of premature death are common.

Many girls report, "Something very bad happened to me." Yet, they hesitate to share with their friends. They get the idea that friends are fearful it will happen to their moms. Even for the girls who had loving surrogate mothers in the form of grandparents, aunts, or a loving father, there is often the tangible tension of their families' collective sorrow lurking just under the surface. This can be felt and can influence emotions, philosophy of life and behaviors, even when there are positive and loving role models and competent caretakers.

In *Time Bomb*, a novel by Jonathan Kellerman, there was a clear illustration of what happens when there is early childhood loss with repressed anger and mental confusion. The loss (death) of a boyfriend was especially traumatic to a woman who experienced the death of her mother at age 5. She grew up to be fearful, closed herself off from the world and withdrew. When she was a child, she was unable to grieve, and the sorrow just sat there and festered. She stopped trusting and learned to fear the world. Since she became a loner, her boyfriend was the first person who tried to relate to her. He became a substitute parent. She looked up to him and slowly began to come out of her shell and learned to trust again. When he died, all her repressed emotions were triggered and began to explode. Her reaction was so intense, she needed intense professional treatment.

Daughters and Loss of Mother through Adolescence

Many of the women in this age group who lost mothers had difficulty with verbal and self-expression. They became better listeners than talkers. When a woman was in elementary school, her class project was to make cards for their Mother's Day celebration. She reports, "I could not make a card. I felt different, permanently marked as defective. Her death defined me." These girls can remember the time before the death when they felt comfortable, cared for, and loved. They have the memory of helping their mother to cook, standing on a chair next to her. This was referred to as the 'good times.'

Jane, a woman who lost her mother when she was only seven, reports that it is still difficult to ask for help or to allow others to do anything for her. She is a caretaker of her young family, yet yearns for her own mother to tell her, "You are such a good mother." Jane reports that when she is upset or stressed, she finds herself acting like a 7-year-old. She becomes obsessive, fearful, and distrustful. She is sure no one will take care of her needs and keep her safe.

Joyce, at age 37, wrote a poem when her daughter attended nursery school. She also lost her mother when she was seven, and this poem so eloquently and aptly describes her emotions.

Nursery School

What thoughts I have of you each morning, Mom, as I carry Samantha, named to honor your mother, into nursery school.

What courage leaving home at just-turned three. Red-rimmed eyes. Security blankets trimmed to manageable squares. Tiny fingers clenched round pant legs.

Your granddaughter rhythmically strokes Bunky Bear's brown fur, straying onto the bare patch on his chest, sucking her "tall man" and "ring man" 'till they're calloused. But now she demands a new Bunky, her love object too easily replaced.

Open tubs of Play-Doh beckon. Chunky crayons roll off the table. The teacher reaches out her hand, a bridge from Mother to school.

We call her independent, strong-willed, determined, and what she wants is me. I must kiss her on top of her head, hug her as I count to ten, then wait for her kiss upon my cheek.

Her comfort rituals – and mine. Prodding each lock with a knife to be sure the connection will hold, clicking each light switch three times at light's out. Traces of obsessive-compulsive behavior are not surprising, explains a therapist, for a girl-turned-woman whose Mother died when she was seven.

In room 206, white paper cats with finger-painted polka dots dance from the clothesline. Ballerina lunchboxes cradle their peanut butters and jellies. Paper bag owls see all.

It's November and still she sobs when I leave. I take too long to say goodbye, her teacher suggests. "Just say 'I'll be back;' that's the key. Smile and reassure. I'll be back."

But you left, Mom, and you didn't come back. Thirty years ago you left me – and you never came back.

Little wonder that I linger now.

Joyce E.

Daughters and Loss of Mother in Teen Years

The teen who understands finality feels more turmoil. There might be a harboring of guilt because her mother died during a time when their relationship may have been tense or troubled. When a teenager loses her mother, she feels robbed of the opportunity to redefine their relationship from the turbulent teen years. She feels cheated out of an adult relationship with her mother. She frequently feels a loss of trust. Some say they become fearful of saying "Good-bye" to people, afraid they might never see them again. Each woman realized she hangs onto the people in her adult life forever. Many have trouble separating from people, even when the relationship is no longer viable.

Some girls refuse to participate in the same sports or hobbies that their mother enjoyed, and feared a competition with her. If they were told, "You are going to be just like your mother," it meant, "I would be dead." There was the feeling of "I can't grow up." Every life change felt like a small death because their mother is gone. Many have said: "Every new stage reveals my defect – I do not have a mother. Her death froze our relationship and ended my childhood and normal development."

There will be no going through milestones or life cycles together. There will be no mother-daughter struggles and no aging parent to care for. Many girls grow up feeling very vulnerable. When they grow to adulthood without their mothers, they report, "There is a loss of the mirror that marks my current age. If my Mom did not age, how can I?" There is this fear that death will occur at the same age as their mother. When she lives past that dreaded age, she notes "I've outlived my mother by so many years." Then life goes on and the mother is not there to help with, acknowledge, appreciate or share her own life, her daughter's life or the lives of the next generation. There is no one to replace one's mother. There is the absence of a cheerleader, someone to say "You can do it." It is difficult to find one's identity without a mirror, mentor, or provider of unconditional love and acceptance.

Some women who lost their mother as teenagers recall how they felt like they had to stifle their own loneliness and sadness in order to keep their father's love. Many felt a need to protect him from his own expressions of grief. They had a sense that their father was unable to deal with his own emotions, and therefore, could not possibly deal with theirs. Often there is a feeling of rage, a loss of self-esteem or a feeling of being flawed. After some therapy and grief work, many describe how they see themselves as survivors. Each feels a distinct need for a mother, yet becomes a caretaker for their father, siblings, and then their own family. Each woman could retain the feeling no one is there to take care of her. When upset, stressed or fearful, each tends to regress back to the age she was at the time of her loss. She tends to feel that her mother's death shaped her life.

Many women fear other people's anger. Many feel anger in their daily life and realize it is not due to the present moment but coming from a deep and empty place inside. There is a belief it is impolite for one to speak of her loss or make others feel uncomfortable. Many women feel that all they became in life, as well as all they failed to accomplish, can be traced back to their early loss. Grief is unspoken and ignored publicly and socially. It is only with others in the "Dead Parent Club" where an intimate kinship quickly emerges and deepest shared pains are safely exposed and for one brief moment – shared. There is a feeling that "loss is forever," "loss is character," "loss is muse," and "loss is a way of life." When asked by others who recently lost a parent, "When does it stop hurting?" those in the "Dead Parent Club" answer, "If it ever does, I'll let you know." We never forget those we lose and we continue to be influenced and shaped by them and the effects of that loss all of our lives.

Many women can describe themselves as being happy and outgoing before the loss of their mother and as insecure and fearful of abandonment afterward. There are many fears of future losses. If a mother left before the birth of the grand babies, there is a longing for what might have been. There is also the extreme sadness of having to raise her children without her mother's input, especially hearing, "You are a good mother." There might be anger toward her husband for not being a good parent to her. There is often a tendency to feel a lack of grounding and this could result in the woman needing to feel in control of everything in her life. If everything is not in a particular order, she might feel anxiety. She could also feel anxious when there are changes and surprises even in small ways. Often when seeing mothers and daughters together, there are feelings of sadness, regret and tears.

Fears of abandonment often dominate, and the reaction is to become dependent on others. Seeking large amounts of affection and social interaction can come from growing up not feeling safe, happy, protected, secure and sheltered. Young women have described how they were naïve about the realities of life. Some fear they put too much neediness on their husband and children. Those who feel abandoned, hurt, angry, terrified and empty often become overweight. Food is used to fill one up and one then feels less empty and is comforted. An over abundance of comfort foods also numb the pain and sadness. Eating keeps feelings from surfacing. Compulsive overeating can lead to eating disorders, which then take on a life of their own, creating real health issues. Many of these women are faced with lifelong depression. Another difficult aspect of parent loss is the need to move to another home, such as to the home of a grandparent or other relative. This often means a move to another town, a new school and the need to make new friends at a time when they are at their emotionally weakest and most vulnerable. This leads to feelings of loneliness and one feels like an outsider. Even as adults, these women report that it was difficult for them to maintain their adult relationships, causing them to have many marriages and divorces.

Many teenage girls feel they have to grow up too quickly. There are often household tasks, shopping, meal preparation, the caretaking of younger siblings, and perhaps, being a surrogate wife to Father. These young women felt that their father's grief filled a universe. This created a lack of place for the children to express their grief. They had no support system, no attention and no sympathy or empathy. Growing up feeling cheated, many said they "had to scratch out a life in order to survive." There was the feeling of envy for other girls who had their moms. There is sadness within those who have had no adults available to them. There is often a feeling of not being nurtured. Feeling alone, especially all the years they needed their mother, they tend to use food or other substances as comfort, suffer from eating disorders, or other health issues due to substance abuse or other addictive behaviors. They, therefore, tend to create a protective wall around themselves.

Daughters and Lost of Mother in Early Adulthood

Amy, a 47-year-old woman, lost her mother in her early 20s. Her mother became ill at the age she is now. Being ill for two years, she passed away at 49 on Amy's second wedding anniversary. She and her mother had been best friends. Amy was very involved with her mother's care, working desperately to help find the right doctors, the best treatment and to find a cure. While ill, her mother was stoic and never complained. She had been the center and strength of her family, and she continued to remain strong for her daughter and younger son. Her illness was never discussed with her family. Amy tried to make her mother's last days as pleasant as possible, and felt very alone.

The effect of her mother's death was intense anger for many years. The loss caused Amy complete despair. Her mother was her strength and support, always supporting her feelings and encouraging her life choices. As her main cheerleader, Amy felt her mother loved her more than anyone ever could. Amy felt grateful for the unconditional love that her mother was able to provide. Amy knew she and her brother were their mom's only treasures and her only pleasures in life. Before her mom died she wrote beautiful, loving letters to her children. Amy became angry at God and became very bitter.

Having reached this age of her mother's illness, Amy realizes how very young her mom was. She has health risk factors and still struggles with weight issues. She realizes she needs to take control of her life and health, which she has begun to do. She expresses she is overly emotional. Being sensitive, Amy feels hurt a lot of the time. She also cries easily at both sad and happy times, and feels her tears slowly release some bottled up feelings.

When Amy's children were born, the feelings of being cheated were overwhelming. She knew her own children would miss a wonderful and loving grandmother. There was a lot of sadness that her mother was not there to share her joy or to experience the extreme pleasures a grandmother has. Feelings of sadness surface during weddings, showers, births and deaths. Mother's Day is particularly difficult for her. When her children were young, Amy developed a lot of anxiety and fears that limited her life. She was fearful she, too, would die at 49, leaving her own children without a mother. She says she will feel relief once she gets beyond that year. She realizes how very much life her mom missed. Amy reports how she becomes terrified when she or one of her children becomes ill. She fears the death of her loved ones. Amy feels, on some level, she is waiting for it to happen. This is a constant, ever-present pain. She realizes life is so fragile with such a fine line between life and death. Amy says at night, in the dark, she is often overcome with a chill of knowing we do not live forever, and one day we will not be here, and we have no control over it. She worries about the safety and wellbeing of her children.

The sadness of her mother's loss is increased by the sadness of her mother's life, which, Amy reports, was different from the one she hoped to live. Amy says her mom suffered from low self-esteem and always felt she didn't accomplish what she wanted to in life. Amy knew her parents didn't have a happy marriage, so she worked very diligently in her own life to create an atmosphere of a happy and healthy marital relationship. She grew up seeing her mother care more about others than herself. Her mom was a very good caretaker of her own elderly mother, her siblings and her two children. Although her mom's own personal dreams were never fulfilled, she never complained and was never bitter. Amy lived with purpose, trying to make up for all the deficits in her mother's life. She felt she was living for herself and her mother. Amy wanted to live her life to realize her own dreams and get the good parts of life her mother missed. "I am now my mother's legacy."

What has given Amy strength and courage to go on to live a satisfying life was her mother's expressions of love, appreciation and thankfulness for all Amy did and for being the person she is. Her mother wished her all kinds of good luck and good fortune and praised her for being the best daughter in the world. Amy knew her mother was always "there for me – giving me support and approval and guidance." The knowledge that her mother was so proud of her is what sustained her and allowed her to go on. What Amy learned from her mother included, "make yourself happy," "make things be okay," and to have "peace at any cost." She learned how to follow her mother's example of being insightful and knowing how to motivate others to follow their interests. Amy has followed her mother's example by becoming the nucleus of the family.

24

She did it for her mother, as a way to replace as well as honor her. Today, she is the caretaker of her family and others. She learned to be strong and independent so no one would have to take care of her.

Amy has thought about her mother daily and especially on anniversary times and holidays. At the anniversary time of her mother's death, she suffers from bouts of depression. She continues to feel sad about all that her mom and she and her children have missed. The loss continues to be felt. Amy's first daughter was named for her mother. She lives with the belief that "people don't get what they deserve. There are no guarantees." She looks forward to the relief she will feel when she lives past the date of her mom's death. Yet, because Amy knows there are no guarantees, she is unable to see beyond this milestone. She cannot imagine going beyond the age of her mother and often feels doom and depression. She reports that she is doing all she can to care for herself emotionally and physically. Amy believes that her family unit is doing well, and she has a lot of joy in her life. She feels pleased she is able to utilize her skill of making other people feel loved and comfortable. Her children are very important to her and she is their best cheerleader. In order to counter her inner fears, Amy has enrolled in a graduate course to receive her doctorate degree. She hopes to begin a new career, and to live beyond the upper limit she has always seen for herself. This tangible goal will be the beginning of a whole new aspect of life – one not ever expected. She wants to know there is life after 50.

Reflections

It is especially difficult for a woman to grow up without a mother. She loses the mirror, which her mother provides. Without this mirror, she is unsure of who she is, lacking a clear picture of her own identity as a grown woman, wife and mother. She has lost her role model and road map, thereby losing the ability to see herself in the future or picture herself growing old. Many of the young women I interviewed expressed the thought: "If my mom did not age, how can I?"

The young woman often has lingering self-doubts about her ability to be a good mother since she had to do so without her mother's emotional support, encouragement, role modeling and personal praise.

Every woman yearns to hear: "You are doing so well. You are such a good mother." If a daughter has the memory of her mother providing unconditional love, support and acceptance, she is more able to draw from some inner strength and be more resilient and resourceful as she goes through life.

Often the young teen has to take on too much adult responsibility for her grieving father, has to run the household, care for younger siblings, and prepare meals with no one providing support or caring for her own physical or emotional needs. Many times this occurs in a new neighborhood where there is little to no peer, family or community support. Feelings of abandonment, isolation and loneliness continue to overwhelm and overburden. These after-shocks can continue for years.

Part II
Sons and Loss of Mother in Childhood

Loss of a mother in childhood often caused children to be raised by the father and sometimes a stepmother, which can have varying effects depending on many different factors, which will be addressed in the Healing section. Very often the father is unable to cope with childcare and home management. He, therefore, depends on his parents, siblings and other family members. So, the life of the child changes totally. Many have to make many adjustments and cope with changes of location, school, friends, house rules, grief of the father, sadness of other family members plus their own grief, sadness and fear. Many times the young boy had to keep all of his feelings to himself, all mementos a secret. Many felt guilty for having feelings and sadness because most never had fathers or family members able to speak of their loss. They were denied any expression of their mother. For many there is the memory of how their inner and outer worlds fell apart when their mother died. Her loss represented the end of safety and security. Some say they felt they lost their confidant. For many youngsters, losing the one who took very good care of them caused them to grow up feeling angry and fearful. They claim early experiences shaped their attitudes, values, desires and choices. Many vowed to have a marriage that would be stable and strong. The highest value was placed upon the person who would be the mother of their children.

26

Michael, a young writer, spoke of losing his mother as a young child. He reports having had a grim childhood. He refers to his mother in his writings; he speaks of loss of the first love and other childhood sorrows. He spoke of shattered dreams. His writing is a way to search for his own history, identity and legacy. This inspirational speaker lost his mother at a young age and always felt a sense of urgency to help others. He says he feels his mother's presence, and this provides a sense of power to continue his career.

The young child who loses a parent lives life with this loss and believes he is shaped by the loss. It is who he is: "A person who lost my mother." Often one feels he is not a complete person and continues to see himself as if he were still a "5-year-old," etc. regardless of his chronological age. Loss often pervades every aspect of his life, affecting self-image and causing him to be overly concerned with the image he projects on others. For one youngster, his maternal grandmother helped him to heal by the bond they created with each other. She shared his sadness and loss. His mother's death was out of natural sequence for his grandmother, who lost her only daughter. His loss occurred at an age when he needed his mother so much. He and his grandmother created the comforting ritual of preparing holiday meals together. Their mutual sadness and empathy for each other led to their creative food preparation and sharing with extended family.

Most boys feel they are shaped by the loss of their mother. They say that all they become and much of what they fail to become can be traced directly and indirectly to this loss. Jason, a man who lost his mother to murder when he was seven, talked about how, in an instant, he lost his mother and his father was accused and taken to jail. He was devastated and his world forever changed. He felt isolated, stigmatized by other children and was deeply traumatized. He had years of having delusions that he saw his mother everywhere. He grew up with the inability to trust or form relationships. He never married and only began to heal after he joined Murder Victims' Families for Reconciliation. Being able to share with others in similar circumstances became the turning point for him.

Many men spoke of how often they go to the phone to call their mom. They think, "Oh, I have to call Mom and tell her that." The sudden realization that she is not there hits again and again and the familiar pain returns. Alexander, a 30-year-old man, lost his mother when he was 12. He described having a large, painful lump on his upper back. A deep-tissue massage therapist called this "a ball of tension." He remembers having had this lump since his mom's death. His bodywork with the massage therapist led him to feel deep anger at his mom for having abandoned him. He eventually was encouraged to express his feelings and soon realized he was holding onto his mother. After many treatments, Alexander was emotionally ready to let her go. In time the lump of tension dissolved and the physical pain was also gone.

Sons and Loss of Mother in Teen Years

Peter, a 30-year-old businessman, lost his 40-year-old mother when he was 17. He said he was in a "surreal state of limbo." He was comforted by family, friends and his teachers from his small private school and felt appreciation for everyone's concern. Yet, he also felt removed from people, locked inside, feeling a protective wall around him and feeling distant. He interacted with people, heard their words of sympathy and continued with his daily life. Their words were meaningless. He felt that no one could possibly know how it is. The effects of his mother's loss were that he attended a college near home instead of going away to school as he had planned. Peter's religious beliefs were shaken. He felt if God existed, his prayers for her recovery would have been answered. He lost his ability to trust that all would go well. His contentment was destroyed, and he felt his life would not go the way he grew up to believe it would. Peter felt vulnerable, angry and cheated. He expressed that he had been angry and nasty at times and now knows how hurtful these emotions are to himself and the people he loves.

Peter is unable to confide in others, says he still feels different from his peers, and often feels unfortunate but fears the pity of others. He says he had to grow up more quickly and had to become more mature and independent sooner than his peers. Peter believes he is more self-sufficient today and has learned earlier about life. He still has his dreams for the future but says, "We have to accept what life brings and just grin and bear it." His mother had always been emotionally available to him and provided unconditional love. When she passed away, he worried he would not be able to find true love.

At holiday and anniversary times, Peter misses his mother and wishes she were here. He feels he has made choices of which she would have been proud. Today, he has a fiancé who has many qualities similar to his mother. He plans to be married and looks forward to being a father. Now he realizes that people die and life changes. Peter believes he has learned to be kind and is careful not to hurt anyone. As he looks to the future, he fears for his own health and hopes he will live long enough to see his own children grow up.

Reflections

Knowing that a mother is not at home to nurture the child causes a pain that resides deep inside. People who have lost their mothers contain a certain sadness in their eyes and they easily bond with others in their unique sisterhood or brotherhood. Missing their mothers comes at various times and during a wide variety of milestones, especially at times of stress and when struggling with decision-making. A mother is often felt to be a son's first love and true confidant, which intensifies the loss. Many search for the perfect love in order to recreate the original love relationship, which ideally is the love between the mother and her baby and toddler. It is part of normal development to long for the recreation of the glorious attachment to one's mother with its bonding and sense of oneness. This feeling again occurs in later life when one "falls in love." This is when we again experience the bonds of oneness while hopefully maintaining our healthy separateness. When one is able to connect and regain that feeling of love again in a healthy adult relationship, many wounds are then healed.

When one passes the critical time, the age the mother or father was at the time of their death, one no longer fears death in the same way. Many worry more about the death of a spouse, leaving one alone again. Some say their spouse has been a "good parent to me and our children." The spouse is often referred to as "nurturing and caring." There is the fear of the same loss coming around again.

Children of all ages say they always remember how they felt at the time of their parent's loss. Most were unprepared, fearful, angry, sad, empty, and guilt-ridden. They describe how feelings got stuck inside; there were no words, and they felt numb. There was no one to talk to who would understand what they were experiencing. They remember being alone, having no emotional support, and no one to protect or comfort them. The loss was seen as a physical blow from which one does not recover. There is then a real fear of loss happening again. Their sadness can last a lifetime.

CHAPTER 3

Loss of Father

A father's role is to protect and care for his family. Fathers are guides of childhood, the nemesis of adolescents and the examples of how to live grown-up lives. The role of a father is for validation. "You are a worthy person, worthy of my attention and love." When a father leaves too soon, and it is always too soon, the sons and daughters are left to sort out who they are and who their father was. They search for their legacy and try to find something to hold onto. One needs to know one's father in order to more fully know one's self.

There is a realization that in one moment – in a flash – life is now different and will never be the same again. With the loss of the father, common symptoms felt by the child are shock, alienation, guilt and a yearning for remembered yesterdays. The trauma is heartbreaking. Emotional pain reaches one's very core, and all the child wants is for "yesterday to be back again." With alienation, the child feels different from everyone else. He often feels: "No one can understand what I am going through. I am alone." The world as he knew it was no more. His world was turned upside down. The rules of this new life are no longer known.

Adults who lost their father at an early age describe feelings of shame and sadness. There was no longer a father to protect and encourage, and there continues to be a palpable sense of loss. This often leads to poor coping skills, depression, alcoholism and other addictions, including being a workaholic. The child grows up thinking, "Where is my father?" Some feel they were responsible for their father's death and feel the need for self-punishment or fear God will punish them. Others grow up believing: "My father sees me, hears me, watches over me. He sees I am successful, and he is proud of me."

Part I
Daughters and Loss of Father

If a father dies when his daughter is young, chances are he will continue to exert a strong influence on her through fantasy. He becomes idealized and perfect as she uses him as the most perfect relationship model, causing frustration since this is mostly an impossible search. A father's role is to mirror back to his daughter that she is valuable, interesting, attractive and female. The daughter needs to know her father views her as feminine. When a woman has the sense that she is able to bestow pleasure on her beloved father, it breeds in her a desire to please men. These are the rewards of the good girl who often needs to do nothing other than exist and she knows her father is pleased with her. She thereby receives safety and approval.

Women who have lost their father often seek father substitutes. This search is largely on the unconscious or subconscious level. Women then seek out people they feel like or value them. They seek this dynamic in work, mentoring and personal relationships. The daughter's relationship with her mother is often fraught with negativity because her lost father is held up on a pedestal and her mother is merely human. If a mother remarries, the daughter's relationship with her stepfather will likewise be negative because he is "not my real father" and his attempts to relate to her will be resisted out of loyalty to her deceased father.

A father's task is also to provide his daughter with feelings of beauty, of being a beautiful and lovable person. His role is to encourage her to identify with her mother, which provides her with her core gender identification. If a father is not there for his daughter, she lacks the feedback and does not know if she is attractive. She might tend to grow up to be attracted to and seek out unavailable men. She might have the need to make these men love her. She often feels a sense of low self-esteem or feels devalued. She seeks the attention, affection and admiration of those who are unavailable to her. A woman might also have the need for attachment to a man because she believes or fears she is nothing without a man. Perhaps she is really seeking her daddy. The role of her father was to compliment, value, support and encourage her.

32

Women who grow up with dads who live up to their roles are provided a sense of independence and the ability to achieve a strong personal identification. A father represents the real world outside the house to his daughter. A father is his daughter's key to success in love and work. These women grow up with dads who create a feeling of being safe and secure. They then develop a core belief that they will always be well cared for, safe and secure. Women with these fathers describe how even without money, they never felt poor. Women who lost their fathers describe their anger, hurt, sadness, fear and loss of faith. They describe how their fear of abandonment caused a distrust in the universe. They tend to spend their lives holding on too tightly to the people they love and fear the loss of their loved ones.

Daughters and Loss of Father in Childhood

Anna, a 40-year-old woman, was two when her father died suddenly. She grew up always aware of not having a dad. She refused to attend school or other functions when there were father-daughter themes. As a teenager, she liked boys and became addicted to the most unavailable boy, who was distant, just like her dad who was out there in heaven. In college, she felt a lack of guidance and had no awareness of how the world or life worked. Anna became depressed and felt that life is too painful. She had a difficult time forming a relationship. The unavailable men rejected her. She had fears of both engulfment and abandonment. She finally married a much older man who was a father substitute. He made all her decisions, and she eventually felt she was disappearing. Being in therapy enabled her to divorce, find her stronger self, and create a life with a purpose.

Sandra, a 49-year-old woman, lost her 55-year-old father when she was 8 1/2. He had been ill for five months and spent a lot of that time in the hospital. She and her 14-year-old brother were at home with an elderly, somber aunt while her mother was at the hospital, which was approximately two hours away. An older sister was away at college. The atmosphere in the home was filled with intense emotion. Her mother became overly stressed and yelled a lot, was distracted and upset. The day-to-day living was in crisis mode. When Sandra had to stay at the home of other relatives, she felt displaced. When her father was able to be at home, he was too ill to interact with her, and she felt rejected. No one explained anything to her. She did not understand how ill he was, did not know he was in pain and did not know he was going to die. She went to sleep one night and woke up to learn he died during the night and was gone. He had been taken away while she slept. She was awakened to the sound of her brother crying. After she cried, she went numb. She was taken to the funeral home, but not to the cemetery. Everything was a blur. Sandra felt that no one cared about her, and this left her feeling isolated, resentful and angry.

While everyone was at the cemetery, Sandra was alone in her room. When people returned to the house, she did not want to talk to anyone. She felt that no one could possibly understand what she was experiencing. Sandra felt she was different from everyone else and that she was never going to be the same again. She reports that she believed "none of our lives would ever be the same again." During the week of Shiva, (the week of mourning), she saw her older sister being verbally defiant, saying what she wanted to say. Sandra said: "She became my hero. I hated everyone who came to the house to pay their respects. I wanted to know why they came, where they were before, and where they would be later. I felt anger and hate."

The silent messages Sandra heard in the week after the funeral were: "No matter how we feel, we have to busy ourselves with the people who came to the house." She saw her family preparing food and serving even though they were unhappy about it. She does not remember anyone talking to her or attempting to comfort her. She knew something terrible had happened and there was no turning back. She remembers feeling "I must help Mom because she is overburdened and unable to cope. She yelled and made me feel I was killing her." The message was, "If you don't do what someone wants, they will die."

In dreams, her dad was only away and coming back. He was not really dead – this was a mistake. He was only far away – yet he could never get back. She had these dreams for a few years. When her father died, Sandra was in the third grade. Every day she had stomach pains. She cried in the bathroom at school and could not stay there. Since her mom did not drive, she was sent home from school in a taxicab. She was put on a tranquilizer, which made her feel groggy and she felt like she was falling asleep in school. Eventually, the stomach pains subsided and she was able to stay in school. Sandra continued to feel there was a "black mark" on her, and that she was different from everyone else. She resented those who had fathers and believed that life is not fair and there is no justice. Sandra said, "It doesn't matter what you do, bad things will continue to happen anyway."

Since Sandra's classmates were nicer to her than ever before when she finally returned to school, she felt they were being false. She continued to feel alienated, like an outsider. She says she "wrote everyone off" and felt "no one can make me feel better, so why are they even trying." Although she excelled in her school work, she was unable to do her Hebrew school work, which caused her to feel stupid. She felt a total rejection of religion: "If there was a God – he was a stupid one and I wanted nothing to do with him." Even though she continued to excel in her public school work, she never believed she was smart. Teachers and family members expressed that she was smart, yet she still believed that she was fooling everyone.

Sandra's mother was left with no money, and she had to work long hours at a job that was debilitating to her, both physically and emotionally. Sandra continued to feel that she was a burden to her mom. She was either sent to stay with relatives, had a babysitter or stayed at home alone. Before the year was over, her mother became ill and was hospitalized. Sandra expressed the fear she felt that her mom would also die and then "who will care for me?" Life was very serious, and she felt a heavy cloud around her. There was no fun or humor or brightness. Sandra remembers always feeling old beyond her years. There was no mourning period. She feared that her friends were not really her friends and that they did not really like her. She felt different and had resentment for other kids and wanted to tell them: "You don't know how good your life is – you have both parents."

Some positive experiences from that time period were a surprise party for her ninth birthday. Also, she frequently visited relatives in another city who paid attention and showed they liked her. Eventually, Sandra's pain decreased and she got used to the new way things were. She was still angry and cried a lot, but thought she was crying about daily issues. As she grew up, there was no buffer from her mother, who made all the decisions. Her mother was anxious, very emotional, had a lot of self-doubt and floundered in her daily decision-making. Sandra believed her father would have protected her and been a calming and balancing presence to limit the emotional turmoil.

Her career decision was made by default – she went into education and got an MA degree in Education and Counseling. Sandra lacked self-confidence and was never able to perceive of herself as anything other than a teacher. Again, she felt the absence of her father, who might have helped guide and encourage her to achieve her true desire, which was to become a clinical psychologist. She described herself as "a poor kid from the wrong side of the tracks – on a lower rung on the ladder – not on par with the wealthy kids in better neighborhoods." She was influenced by her mother's messages to "just get through the day," and "people plan and God laughs." Just like her mother, Sandra says she never planned for her future, but merely fell into one thing after another. She felt there was no guidance, direction or goals. As an adult, she still sees her life as a function of other people's needs – just as she was a function of her mother's life. She felt it was her job as the youngest child to help her mother in any way she was needed. Sandra learned how to keep her mother calm and happy. She says she believed she could "have my own life in my spare time."

Sandra's health concerns were related to heart disease, which her mother and her mother's family suffered as opposed to the cancer, prevalent in her father and his family. She was also concerned about her husband's health, fearful he would die young and leave her with a child to raise alone, following her mother's fate. Anniversary times were always difficult, especially February when her father and uncle both died (four years apart on the same date). February was just to be gotten through. Sandra always had the fear someone would die in February. Sandra is still a person who distances herself from feelings, which are still too overwhelming and scary. Even to this day, she continues to feel some degree of isolation.

Sandra's memory of her father is that their life together was normal, although he worked late, leaving little time for a lot of contact. He was there every morning to make her breakfast and feed her. Her memory of him is of warmth, sweetness, caring and love. With him she felt loved, cared for and special. She believes that this relationship provided her with the ability to love and be loved. The year her son was eight, the age she was when her father died, she continued to see herself at that age. She became over-empathetic and emotionally involved with her son. She felt his pains and upsets along with him. In a sense, she felt like she merged with him and saw him as herself. Sandra strongly believed if her husband were to die, it would be that year. She also feared she and her husband would die in an accident, and her son would be left alone. Sandra realized how very young eight is to be so traumatized, as she had been. She believes that the severe emotional break that occurred in her loss caused her to lose whoever she might have been – and would be no more.

If her father had lived, Sandra believes her whole personality would have been different. She feels she would have been less harsh, less angry, less moody, less depressed. She was taught that feelings aren't important, and that one should just be cheerful, and just cope. She feels she gets too nasty with her husband and son and that she might have been more able to express herself more directly. Her mother would have been less needy of her because she would have been less burdened. Today, Sandra believes, she would feel less burdened by every day life and might be a better caretaker.

Sandra reports that this experience with the interview process was very intense. She says it "stirred up a lot of old stuff." It also put things in a better perspective, giving her more clarity to see today's issues. She sees that what occurred by her early loss became a lifelong handicap. Sandra continues to live out fears and beliefs acquired at that time as well as the philosophy to just get through the day. She still has to fight the feeling that things will go wrong, that she will be the victim and she will not get what she wants. She still has trust issues, and it is very difficult for her to let people in or to let anyone take care of her.

A daughter grows up wanting her father's approval. If her father is gone, she might develop a condescending or negative attitude towards the men in her life. She might also create or fantasize an "ideal man" who remains forever desired and forever sought in vain. When a father is gone, she could have difficulty sustaining intimacy in relationships. Without a father, she might also question if she is entitled to pursue her own career ambitions or lifestyle choices if they conflict with her father's perceived (or real) expectations. His approval and/or permission are what she seeks.

Some women speak of shame and somatic reactions that lead to illness or of anger expressed as overreactions. For these women there is increased sensitivity. Each time their phone call is not immediately responded to, they are crippled by fears of rejection. Others unconsciously seek father substitutes and end up married to a father-image who is usually a much older man who makes all the decisions. They soon feel as if they have no self left. These women might not realize they have real value. The women who become addicted to unavailable men continue to recreate the distance of the absent or lost father, who is "out there somewhere." Perhaps the daughter never felt she was "daddy's girl." She could become fearful of her sexuality when her father is not there as the nurturer and role model for a healthy male-female relationship.

The role of a father to his daughter is to teach her self-reliance, independence, courage and the ability to deal with the outside world assertively. His encouragement and nurturing enables her to develop higher self-esteem, more empathy and increased social skills with her peers. His presence and participation in her life assists in her development as a female and sets the standards of how she is related to and valued by men in the outside world. Her relationship with her father is her first role model for major lessons about the world of men. She learns how to expect to be treated by men as an adult. Ideally, her relationship with her father will be a healthy one and will provide the positive and loving role model for a healthy adult relationship, where she expects to be treated well.

Judith, a 33-year-old woman, talked about losing her 50-year-old father when she was 10. Her immediate strong and enduring emotions were anger and betrayal. She distanced herself from family members and friends. Her defenses from her pain were self-alienation and isolation, both physically and emotionally. Judith lost touch with the feeling part of the self and felt different. She was the only child she knew who had experienced this kind of loss and she felt ashamed. She kept her feelings bottled up and never told anyone about her father. Judith worked hard to keep his death a secret. Her pervasive belief as she grew up was "life can never be the way I want it to be and I am helpless to do anything about it." She felt powerless to make life changes.

Judith has few memories of childhood. There was no real support system. Her life changed financially and it was the end of any real sense of security. She worried about money – "Will there be enough? When will it run out? What will happen to us? Who will take care of us?" Judith always goes back to the fact that her father died when she was asleep and, therefore, she missed an important transition. She missed saying "goodbye." He was gone when she awoke in the morning. She had no idea what was going on. No one explained anything to her and she was not taken to the funeral (her mother thought she was protecting her) and she didn't go to the cemetery. Judith has no visual image of his coffin, grave, what the "death rituals" were, or how her family grieved. She had no information, no role models, no closure and no opportunity for her own expression of grief. She recalls being unable to breathe, and having all her emotions closed down. She had no words or expression for her feelings. These early physical symptoms later developed into illness as her body processed her unexpressed emotions. Judith had difficulty fully accepting her father's death. Her recurring nightmares were that he was ignoring her. She also thought she saw him on the streets wherever she went. She was never able to say, "My father is no longer alive."

Since her mother was so unable to cope, Judith felt she had to be strong and not upset her. Judith's father had been the one who was social and who brought people into the home. He was kind, gentle and a lot of fun. He had a good sense of humor and made people laugh. After his death, there was no more company, no more fun and no more laughter. Anniversary times are still very stressful. At every life event, she continues to long for her father. Judith wonders about "roads not taken." She believes if her father had lived, she would have received more guidance, developed more self-esteem, and that he would have encouraged and supported her desire to go to college.

Daughters and Loss of Father in Teen Years

Many women who lost their father in late teen years have issues around eating, compulsive or addictive disorders and/or relationship disorders. A woman with an eating disorder might have the notion her father never saw her as a valued adult. Since her father is not there, the daughter feels deprived and empty, needing to fill herself up. She has longing for the daddy who was once there but is no more.

Many women maintain a hope that life will be right again. They seek a return to NORMAL. In order to replace the lost father, many women look to relationships with men who will be "the right one," but these men are not available for any number of reasons. These women set themselves up for repeated disappointment. It is called a repetition compulsion. There is the belief that one is entitled to this perfect relationship and actually believes that it can happen. Of course, it soon falls apart, leaving the woman sad, depressed and eager to run away into her own particular addiction or compulsive behavior. Therefore, many turn to overeating or other addictive disorders. The goal is to numb the pain and fill up the empty place inside, which of course, no addictive behavior and no amount of food can fill up.

Often there is the one special relationship some women find, which is a return to a happy time that feels like a "coming home." This relationship often provides the adoration that matches her father's. It feels like a return of that beloved father on a deep emotional level. Sometimes feelings of safety, security and stability are also perceived. Sometimes these relationships work out well and a lot of wounds from the past are healed. Often, there is no return to that happier childhood place when she was "Daddy's girl." Then disillusionment takes place and the hunt for the perfect mate begins again.

The teenager still feels like a "fatherless child." She often reports that she spoke to him in her head. She had not yet become an adult in his eyes, and they never had conversations about the adult world. She imagined how they would speak of world events and politics. She wondered how he had done such a perfect parenting job and wonders how she will do as a parent when her time comes, especially without his input.

Alice, a 50-year-old woman, reported her father died at age 49 and realized he never lived to see 50. She is surprised to realize how very young 50 is, and how much family life is going on that he missed. When she tried to think about her future, she hit a blank wall. Alice is having a difficult time imagining herself living past the point he did. He, once her guide, is no longer ahead of her. She is now "on my own – at the head of the line, part of the next group to die."

Allison, a 23-year-old woman, was 20 when she lost her father. She describes how she lost her sense of security when he died. She feels she became less secure within herself, more vulnerable, more withdrawn and less social. Having been very dependent on her father, she is fearful of losing someone again. Allison also fears being dependent on anyone, and believes she has to do it all herself. She no longer feels well cared for and safe. Allison says her father took charge and he made everything be okay. She feels she has already experienced the worst, yet she keeps herself inaccessible to deep relationships. She is fearful of ever loving someone again. Knowing that the healing process takes time, she is trying to heal herself and is learning to nurture herself to become more secure and more able to trust again.

Dana, a woman who lost her father suddenly as a teenager, suffered shock, sadness and grief. She was the youngest of eight siblings. Her family was supportive of her because they knew she would be devastated. She was "Daddy's girl" and was always treated in a very special way. Dana was lonesome for him at her wedding and when her child was born. Her mother's message was "You don't question why – it has to be the way it is." She felt she became stronger when she saw her mother as emotionally strong. Her father's death brought her closer to her mother and her siblings. Dana's daily life did not change, she went on, kept busy and always did whatever had to be done. She is a caretaker for others and becomes depressed when she is not busy. She demands a lot from herself and cannot tolerate failure in anything she does. She feels she had to become an adult prematurely – jumping from being a dependent child to an adult in an instant. She has taken on her father's caretaker, advisor roles.

The following poem was written by a young woman in her teen years to show her love for her father and his love for her.

THE APPLE

I was the apple of my Daddy's eye, full of love and happiness. Are you really surprised?

Born on a Friday, just six pounds and some, guess what: he wasn't disappointed I wasn't a son.

Now all dressed in pink lace and things, my Daddy looks down and gives me one of his sly little winks. With a toss to the air and a bounce on his knee, I shower him with kisses, and his heart fills with glee.

Shadow to shadow, I follow him wherever his feet may lead, and when I peek up I can see he is well-pleased. Why not? For I am his bright-eyed apple who could set his heart at ease.

With all the love he had to be shared, throughout our days, it is uncompared. For I loved him then as I do today, and believe it or not, it has grown stronger as I go my own way.

For I carry the smile that was upon his face on his last day. Plainly saying that his time here with me was truly not a waste.

In Memory of Willie D.

Yvonne W.

06/08/1977

Sherrie, a 40-year-old woman, says she sees herself as a protector and caretaker of others. Yet, she also feels she needs protection. Being family-oriented, she is the one who gets the family together for holidays and special occasions. She spoke of the ongoing stress that occurs at the anniversary date of her father's death. She has always become ill the month of the loss. Sherrie's most stressful year was when her daughter turned 14, the age she was when she lost her father. Her daughter inadvertently caused her to feel abandoned, alone, fearful and anxious, which is how she felt after her father's death. She reports being a pack rat

– keeping old, useless things, not letting go of anything – always holding on to too much. Being a worrier and fairly obsessive, Sherrie says that she raised her children with a lot of fear and caution. She believes that as soon as you look away for a moment or let your guard down – get relaxed – feel safe – then the bad things happen. Before you know it – everything changes forever. Sherrie suffers from anxiety and many fears, one of which is about her health. She believes she has become like her father with his same health issues of heart disease. Sherrie is kept awake at night with worry, overeats for comfort and smokes. She is now in therapy and trying to help herself make some changes.

My Story – Part II

My father, age 55, died after a brief illness of only four months while I was in my first semester away at college at age 18. He had cancer, which had already metastasized. For the previous two years, I feared and had believed he was ill, but he refused to see a doctor. When he finally did, it was too late. My mother and other relatives had failed in their efforts to encourage him to seek medical attention. They then prevailed upon me to do it. I felt like a failure and blamed myself for a long time because I couldn't get through to him no matter how hard I tried. When he was finally diagnosed and put on strong chemotherapy, no one talked about his illness, no one reached out to comfort him or each other. We lived in a shroud of SILENCE.

I saw my father, a robust man, waste away to well under 100 pounds in four short months. He was unable to eat, so my brain associates lack of appetite, lack of craving or eating enjoyment to starvation leading ultimately to death. One of the many fears I suffer from is the fear of being skinny or even very thin. I fear not being able to eat, and wasting away.

As an immigrant, he had no formal education. As the oldest child, I was the first to go to college. I had looked forward to going away to school, and one of the major plans both he and I had was for him to drive me and be there with me for my first day. We talked about it and both planned for it and looked forward to this big day we would share together. When it came time to leave, I was told that my uncle would be taking me. My dad was too ill to make the long trip. I no longer felt like I wanted to leave for school and lost all interest in college. I felt trapped and forced to continue what I felt was a charade. I felt my parents had not been honest with me; I was being sent away and I knew in my heart things would not be okay, even though I was told "everything will be okay." I said "good-bye" to my father at the front door. We hugged and kissed and we each said, "I love you" for the last time. I arrived at school still tearful and sad. At school, I only wanted to be home. A month later, I got the call that he was gone.

Some of my memories from his illness are:

(1) Seeing him at the kitchen table unable to eat while he and our family pretended everything was normal.

(2) Feeling I had to entertain him and distract him with stories, which he enjoyed.

(3) Seeing him in the hospital where he was so depressed, sad, and in pain. Knowing my presence there brought him pleasure, seeing his eyes open, seeing him smile at me, and hearing him call me his "shayna madela" (beautiful girl) made me feel less helpless. At least I was able to bring him a bit of pleasure, and that became my major goal.

When I returned home from school after the dreaded early morning phone call to notify me to come home because my Dad was very ill, I knew inside that he had already died. I was immediately faced with the covered mirrors, which signified a death – I was therefore informed – without words. My silent messages from my mother were that I was expected to keep myself together, not fall to pieces or become too emotional. I gulped down my tears and my feelings and felt numb and all alone. I had no comfort from my mother or any of the many relatives who had already filled the house. Some comfort came from a few friends, but mostly I felt myself watching, becoming an observer and not a part of my grief experience. I felt I could not be comforted because I followed my mother's detached affect. I felt it was all surreal. I went through the motions, did whatever was expected of me and all I could feel was anger at everything that was happening and at all the rituals of this time and especially at God.

I recall wondering if I would survive the funeral. I kept feeling faint and was given smelling salts to revive me. I have no memory of who belonged to the woman's hand breaking open and holding out the smelling salts to keep me on my feet. My association with this moment, which came only after writing this book, is that this feeling (and fear) of not being able to "stand on my feet," both literally and figuratively, followed me throughout my life, coming at times of stress and fear, which often have lead to anxiety. My association with receiving the smelling salts led to my carrying a "symbolic smelling salts" in the form of medication such as Valium. I carried them in my purse from that day forward replacing them when they get too old. I never took any of the medication, just used them as a crutch. Knowing they were available was enough to calm me. I also studied and practiced various breathing and relaxation techniques through my life, which I have always preferred to medications.

I recall feeling some comfort when I saw the large number of people who had come to pay their respects. Everyone was crying and I remember noticing that although it was February and there was a lot of snow, the sun was shining and the air felt warm. This was remarkable in a town that experienced winter from October to April. I thought this was the least God could do for us.

I knew that financially we were not very well off. My dad was in business with my uncle, but it was a modest business, and my mother didn't work until after his death. I can recall never feeling deprived, but I was also aware that my wants and needs were very meager. I had the idea that I would always be taken care of and I would always have enough. I got that belief from always being well taken care of by my dad even though there was little available money. He had instilled in me an optimism for life and a belief that he would always be there to take good care of me and that things would be good. I was in for a rude awakening. My mother had to work and I saw how difficult this was for her. I had to borrow money to continue my education and by the end of my freshman year, my mother became ill and I had to move back home, help care for my younger siblings and help with the house. I commuted to another college 25 miles away.

As a freshman in college, immediately after my dad's death, I returned to school wearing the torn black ribbon that Jewish people are to wear for the first month after such a loss to signify the tearing of the loved one from our lives. I felt shame wearing this ribbon on my shirt, so I wore it inside my clothes, on undergarments so it could not be seen. I was unable to tell people what happened and kept my dad's death a secret. Only my boyfriend (soon to become my husband) knew about it. I felt "something was wrong with me" because my father had died. I also felt abandoned, like an outcast, different, flawed, tainted, embarrassed and ashamed, as well as very angry. I felt no one would understand what I was going through. One evening I met a girl who had the exact same experience, having lost her father the same month as I. I met this girl in my college dorm, and we talked and shared our stories long into the night. We shared a bond of understanding, intimacy and sisterhood. Then, I never saw this girl again. Her disappearance was so abrupt that I felt exposed and abandoned and my shame increased. It took me twenty more years before I was ever able to openly discuss the losses of both my parents and this was when I began individual therapy, and later, group therapy. This was also when I was in my graduate program to become a therapist. It took me 20 years to begin my mourning/grieving process.

As an 18-year-old, my losses (and the losses of many of the people I interviewed) included loss of innocence, of trust, of faith, of security, of safety, of direction, of stability, of the future.

My faith in God and in life was shaken. I realized that nothing made sense anymore. It was a confusing time and I felt I was on the sea without an anchor. We lost a sense of family and of "home." We became people who were floundering with no one to take care of us. My belief was "if there is no father, there is no family." Everything became meaningless and I felt sad all the time.

Wondering how my life might have been different had my father lived, I believe I would not have had the need to rush to marry the same week I turned 20, while I still hadn't finished college. I might have felt more secure and taken care of and more grounded. I might have really enjoyed my education and perhaps even had a career right out of college. I have no regrets because I have three wonderful children who were born while I was still young and I have had the pleasures of being a fairly young grandmother. I always have felt fortunate to be able to enjoy these treasured gifts, which are the real rewards of my life. I had the sense of urgency to live as fully and as quickly as I could. I am grateful for that.

I grew up totally dependent on my dad. I was the quintessential "Daddy's girl." When he passed away, I was devastated and missed him with every fiber of my being. Not a day goes by when I don't think about him. My deepest regrets are that my father was not alive to enjoy my children with me. All of our lives would have been richer. I also would have been able to more fully enjoy life's milestone events without missing him and without feeling we were all cheated. I have worked very hard to be open with my feelings and to be mindful about the mental and physical realms of life. I have learned to focus on my mind and body, knowing how they are intertwined and doing my best to stay in the best health I possibly can.

Reflections

It is common for daughters who lost their father to describe their new life without him as one without joy and filled with great sadness. Many see it as the end of family life. Many mothers who are left retreat into cocoons of grief and silence and have little or no communication with others. The children are left to live in a haze, deadened inside, isolated and lonely. There is a feeling of increased responsibility in the areas of helping to care for younger siblings, doing household chores or earning money to help make up for the deficits. Many describe lack of security, safety and guidance. They speak of having no role model or road map for their future. There is fear of also dying young. Many daughters see their father as a "guardian angel" who will guide and protect. Some even pray to their father, seeing him as merged with God. Some fear the death of their husband, which would leave them to raise their children alone.

Many describe how shock and grief were all-consuming. Some say they felt like lepers at school – different from the other kids – the only one this ever happened to. Many became insecure and fearful. They worried constantly about something happening to their mother, wondering "will my mom be there when I get home from school?" To this day, they often worry and fear the worst will occur. For many, family is the most important part of life. Some women say that when their father died, they felt a lack of wholeness and fantasized he would come back and put the family together again. They each do everything they can to create wholeness and family togetherness with their husband and children.

Part II
Sons and Loss of Father

The Masculine Mystique, written by Frank Pittman, M.D. and printed in The Networker, May/June of 1990, addresses the topic of masculinity. "In therapy, men want to be able to talk about their failure to get close to their fathers. Boys need masculinity models. They need a road map to become men. They need men in their lives. It is the father who teaches masculinity – what it means, how it is handled and how much is enough. To be a role model, the father has to be present and the boy learns who he is from his father. He can then correct the faults he sees in his father." If a father is gone, the boy feels a lack of this role model and a lack of acceptance. This feeling of acceptance is an essential part of growing into manhood. "If the father is dead, the boy invents any mythology that suits him. He can imagine his father's acceptance or he can spend his life seeking it. He seeks and craves acceptance, love and approval from his father. However, he can also feel rejection in the silence." A mother cannot teach a boy to be a man. She can only point him in certain directions. It is his dad who shows him how far he should go. The dad's job is to teach his son how to be a man with women. A boy needs his father to tell him his masculinity is "quite splendid enough," and he needs to know his father sees him as a competent person and in time, a competent man.

A son longs for his father and anything his father owned becomes charmed. By adolescence, a boy wants to be seen with his father and not his mother. He wants to hang out with his father, wear similar clothes, and do men things. He tries to "fill his father's shoes." He needs his father to protect him from coming completely under his mother's control. He fears femaleness will be contagious and doesn't want it to rub off on him. If his father is gone, he looks to older boys, and might become too daring, doing dangerous things to gain their acceptance. The less that is known about his own father or adequate grown male role models, the more extreme the acts become in hopes of being masculine enough. He looks to TV and movies, and learns to play a role rather than find his authentic self.

Fatherless sons don't know who they are internally. Part of them has not grown up. Albert, a 30-year-old man who lost his father when he was 6 years old, reports he "never had a realistic understanding of what it was to be a man." He also didn't know what a man/woman relationship was about. A boy needs to know his father in order to more fully know himself. Often when a father dies, the mother becomes depressed. The child, usually the son, has to fill the void. He is often told that he now has to "become a man and take care of mom." He grows up overcompensating for the early loss. He is put in the position of needing to be more responsible, and never goes through the normal stages of adolescence and teenage rebellion to learn who he is. He often becomes a surrogate parent to younger siblings. (Of course, this could happen to girls also.)

As an adult, a man might do what he can to keep himself distant from his own child. He feels he lacks the skills for fathering, as if it were a native language he was never taught. He knows he is just making it up as he goes along. His views of manhood were either imagined, secondhand, or dysfunctional. He does things to be like the father of his fantasy or even the one he remembers, but he still suffers from self-doubt.

Sons and Loss of Father in Childhood

Ron, a 30-year-old man, remembers hugging his father for the last time when he was four; his father was leaving for Vietnam and never returned. His father's name is on the Vietnam Memorial, and Ron went to see it. While there, he met other young people who also lost their fathers in their young childhood years. These people from all across the country shared their experiences and their emotions. They expressed how grateful they felt for the opportunity to talk with others of their generation whose lives were so affected by this war. They had the opportunity to express a loss that had been bottled up. Ron, who lost his father at four, misses what he never had, but inside he is convinced that his father loved him and was proud of him. He misses him, yet does not really remember him.

Tom, a 28-year-old man, was six when his 43-year-old father died suddenly of a heart attack. His death was exactly four years after the death of his father's best friend and business partner. The 6-year-old boy was in extreme shock and very frightened. No one was emotionally available to Tom because everyone else was also in shock, and in their own pain. Everything was in total chaos. He saw his father's body being carried away and heard his mother scream and cry. No one explained anything to him and he wasn't taken to the funeral. He never got to say a final good-bye. Tom was ignored by everyone, and given toys to play with. He remembers playing with matchbox cars and staying out of everyone's way. On that day, a speech impediment began. He then stuttered for most of his life. Emotion was caught in his throat and he was paralyzed with fear. Even with speech therapy, Tom still frequently stutters. He recalls feeling ashamed and different from other children when he finally returned to school.

Tom never mourned for his father until his 20s and still asks, "Why?" He still feels the pain of this loss, and still believes on some level that "Daddy is my guardian angel." Tom says he always felt some confusion, and the family never spoke about it. He grew up with few friends. He felt there had been an implicit promise of the way life was supposed to be, should have been, and never was. He still feels cheated and believes his whole life would have been different had his father lived. Tom misses him and still says "if only …." He has elevated his father to a God-like perfect person who would have had unconditional love and acceptance for him. He believes he has suffered due to the lack of guidance his father would have provided.

Tom's fantasy is that he and his father would have been in business together, that he would have been popular, and his life would have been easier. He wouldn't have had to worry about losing his mother, and he wouldn't have been lonely. He longed for a good-father figure to provide a positive loving role model and guide him in development of social skills. Recently, he became more health conscious, stopped smoking, keeps his weight down, and exercises. Tom works with cars and collects model cars because his only real memories of his father include looking at real cars, identifying them, and playing toy cars together. Tom worries that he will also pass away at 43 and says he will breathe easier once he is past that milestone.

Ken, a 36-year-old man, lost his 36-year-old father when he was eight years old. He now has an 8-year-old son with whom he recently developed an intense and conflicted relationship. In his therapy, it was recognized that Ken was now the same age as his father at the time of his death. Ken realized he was having an "anniversary reaction." He was experiencing a reactivation of buried emotions surrounding the loss of his own father at the same age his son is now. He re-experienced the associated feelings of anger, anxiety, and loss. Ken focused his emotional energy on his son and became very reactive to his son's behaviors. Because of the intensity of Ken's reactions to signs of his son's difficulties, his son's negative behaviors escalated.

When Ken's father died, he had to take responsibility and leadership to help his mother and to try to fill his father's shoes. He had to become a little man at the age of 8, didn't get to be a kid, and didn't get taken care of. Ken spent a lifetime of over-functioning and worrying about other family members. Because of this background, he was quick to react to the first signs of irresponsible behavior or incompetence in his son. He was unable to allow his son to be a kid and just have fun. While receiving professional help, Ken realized all this and was able to share with his son how he felt when he lost his father at the age of eight. He shared how angry, sad and frightened he was, and how seeing his son at age eight brings back those old feelings. He also realized that arguing with his son was how he escaped the emotional pain. Being angry at his son kept him from feeling sad about his own loss of his dad. Ken and his son were then able to develop a better understanding of the situation and came up with a plan to work out their own issues.

Joe, a 40-year-old man, had a 10-year-old daughter who is now the same age he was when his father died. Since he doesn't have a role model for family life or for a father-daughter relationship, he is unsure of ways to interact, make decisions, and solve problems. Many men see their greatest accomplishments as being able to build a strong family unit. They feel grateful for their wife and children. Many think more about their own father when the children are born and when they reach the age when the loss occurred. The biggest fear many expressed is that they will not be adequate fathers to their own children. They sense the lack of a model for this role and have no "fatherly advice" to draw upon. There is the worry about not being good enough. Many wonder what legacy was missed: "What do good fathers pass on to their sons?" Some men grow to adulthood and take on many aspects of their own fathers – their political views, ways of life, sense of humor, sports interests, hobbies and their types of business. Early parent loss precludes any of this. The sons were left to forge their own way, learn from doing, and always wonder if their father would have been proud.

David, a 34-year-old man, was 11 when his father died. He resented his father for his death. He felt overwhelmed by having to do everything on his own and missed the support and guidance, which his mother was unable to provide. He felt his path through his teen years and early adulthood would have been easier if his father had lived. David recalls feeling shame and felt he was different growing up without a father. He became "man of the house" and was a support to his mother. He created a daydream fantasy that his father was a secret foreign agent and that he would return home. He longs for his father to be alive and feels this on a visceral level.

David became a news junkie because he and his father always read newspapers together. He wants to accomplish a lot and do something worthwhile. He believes he is a more sensitive person because of his loss. David became a high school teacher, following in his father's footsteps. A memory that continues is seeing a friend at his father's funeral. This memory still overwhelms him with appreciation. He says he will "love this friend forever."

Sam, another young man was also 11 when his filmmaker father passed away. He reports that he still thinks about his father as "Daddy." At some level he says he still feels like that 11-year-old boy. He filled in the blanks and learned a lot about his father and the man he was. He, too, followed in his father's footsteps and works in film.

Sons and Loss of Father in Teen Years

Steve, a 60-year-old man, was 15 when his 45-year-old father died suddenly. He reports that he lost his ability to concentrate and his grades dropped from As to Ds and Fs. His mother had to go to work because of their immediate change in financial status. He was left alone most of the time. Instead of going to college, he joined the Army. His anger and resentment were carried with him, and he can still easily tap into it.

When Steve married and had children, he was determined to put his family's needs first. He was, like his father, a very involved and caring husband and father. Although he has suffered many health issues and feared dying in his 40s as his father did, he has recuperated due to modern medical interventions. Steve has lived his life determined to survive in order to care for his children (and now his grandchildren). When first meeting this very sensitive man, it does not take long before he makes some reference to his early loss and the effects of this loss on his whole life. It lurks just under the surface, always ready to be expressed.

James, a 50-year-old man who lost his 46-year-old father suddenly when he was 16, felt angry at his father for having left so abruptly. There was no chance to say goodbye or to heal the wounds between them. James and his father were in the midst of typical teenage angst. They were having disagreements, heated arguments, many discussions, and their differences were unresolved. He never had a chance to say "I'm sorry," and often wonders if his behavior contributed to his father's death. James remembers that his father was upset before he died. This terrible burden was further complicated by hearing from relatives, "You are now the man of the family. You must be strong for your mother. You must take care of your mother." James described this as being so confusing, since he wasn't even sure who he was. How could he now be the man, the one his mom can count on? He said this was like "picking up a large box and carrying it with him for the rest of his life." He felt a lack of ability to concentrate in school, and he lived in a fog.

James says he "watched life from a remote spot – as if watching life as an observer." Although this "observer feeling" departed after many years and treatment, the "observer shield" came crashing down again at unexpected and stressful times. James reports that to this day "tender father/son scenes in a movie or on television make me teary." He says he even fills with tears during father/son commercials.

Reflections

The son learns who he is, how to grow up to be a man, how to be masculine, and what that really means from his father. Growing up too soon and being expected to be a man and to take care of his mother puts too much pressure on the child and overwhelms him and his development, often changing his path. Some men become withdrawn, never marry and see the dark side of life. All of these people describe how they were unable to concentrate on their schoolwork or careers for many years. They say they were "not themselves," it was like "living in a fog." They were able to "see, hear and speak, but from a removed or remote spot – out of focus – as someone else – everything swirling around as if watching their lives as an observer." They felt they were not really living, merely observing from the outside. This sensation often lasted for a long time. When those sensations dissipate, there are often feelings of grief, sadness, or pain. With professional help and time, these feelings eventually lift in small fragments, and people begin to feel more like themselves again. Then, when least expected – the shield comes down again and the "observer" returns. They reported that as young people, they feared that the sadness and feelings of otherness would continue forever.

When people returned to the home after the funeral to express their condolences, sometimes there would be laughter for a few minutes – and then back to the sadness. The message is: "…even with your worst pain, there can still be laughter." It comes in waves – the sadness, the tears, the laughter – and back to sadness again. Tears and laughter seem to exist side by side. When you allow yourself to feel one – all of a sudden – along comes the other. That is why – for the rest of your life – you feel joy, pleasure, happiness, laughter – and immediately – in the midst – come the tears.

There is also the huge anger – anger for what happened in one's life – at the cards that were dealt. Anger that life will be different now, anger that one's beloved parent had to die while really bad people got to live such a long life, anger that one's own life had to change so much and forever more, and anger that somehow the parent's own behavior caused what happened. The child or teen often fears that perhaps they were somehow responsible for what happened because of what they did or did not do.

CHAPTER 4

Loss of Both Parents

A child needs a mother and a father – two poles to hold the child in place. If one is missing, it is difficult to keep balance. When one or both parents die, the child loses much, including a profound sense of wellbeing, a role model for ideals and standards, a mirror to himself – needed to grow a healthy self-image, as well as the safety of a stable human connection. When a parent dies, one loses his past. The pain remains as a way to stay loyal to the loved one and to keep the memory alive. One often fears that the loss of the pain will diminish the memory and make the parent disappear. The initial reaction might be shock, numbness, disbelief, a disconnected or drifting feeling, shortness of breath, or a feeling of emptiness in the chest area. Although crying helps, one is afraid to cry for fear it will never stop. The grieving person needs assurance that the crying will stop.

Loss of one or both parents has been described by analysts as the most devastating emotional trauma. These are the people most likely to develop serious psychiatric problems and become depressed or suicidal. Even if one has no conscious memory of painful events, the body remembers what the mind represses. Physical symptoms can occur.

The parent who is gone often becomes the idealized, special, most loved person. He or she gets raised to the greatest heights. What we lose before we are ready then becomes the most perfect, and one longs for that which was taken away. Adults who suffered parent loss as a child often had not completed their mourning. Many of these people were arrested in their development and became resistant to change. Symptoms include a confused sense of self. They have difficulty moving from childhood into adulthood and have trouble being successful. They say they feel unable to go on with their education, unable to complete projects or attain career goals.

Complicated grief is when one continues to mourn and has trouble being comforted. They often experience extreme anxiety when separating from loved ones (separation anxiety), post-traumatic stress, or generalized coping disorder. This type of grief increases the risks of developing cancer, high blood pressure, or heart disease. Repressed grief can cause extensive damages physically and emotionally.

Research on early parent loss has shown that some people tend to hold onto emotional pain longer than others, beyond the point when it would be healthier to let it go. These people are more vulnerable to pain and stress and anxiety. The brain can become affected by the traumas suffered, and the person can become hypervigilant and overreactive. Their traumas become a large part of their identity, and they lose a sense of the way the world was before the trauma. They hold onto the trauma to minimize the loss. To let go of it would represent additional loss. When these traumas occur in childhood, a person's entire life can be colored by these effects.

When I lost my mom suddenly at age 61, I was then 31. I didn't think my reaction to her death would be so severe since this was my second loss. However, I was totally consumed by my grief. This, being the second parental loss, actually intensified my reaction, and reenacted my original loss reactions at the same time. It was springtime, the season of rebirth of nature, my favorite time of year. This sudden and shocking loss was compounded by happening on my daughter's ninth birthday. We knew that forevermore she and I would link her birthday to her grandmother's death. We worked hard through the years to downplay the loss and focus on Debbie's birthday, making the day a special one all about her.

Memories are often blocked by our psyches in order to protect us from trauma. My memories from both of my parents' deaths are scant. One memory does persist from my mom's funeral. This is the memory of seeing a large number of people at the funeral home; standing room only, and the room was filled to capacity. I remember thinking: "Mom would have felt good that so many people attended." That night, in a dream, my mom came to me and I recall telling her who all were there to pay their respects. She was, in the dream, very pleased. The funeral was followed by a week of Shiva at my home. I have no memory of that entire week.

I had a difficult time coping with the fact that the world and all the people I knew were continuing to live their usual lives as though nothing had happened. It added to my pain to hear daily casual conversation, laughter, petty complaints, and minor problems. I felt as many others that no one could understand what I was going through. Everything people spoke about felt so unimportant and irrelevant. I felt withdrawn from those around me who had no idea what was happening in my world.

As I coped with the closing up of my mom's dress shop, settled her estate, sold off the contents of our family home, and passed on her belongings to family members, I found there were certain items I was unable to part with, such as her clothing. I took all of her clothes into my home and stuffed them into my already crowded closet. I kept them there for three and a half years and then took them all with me as my family and I moved across the country to Los Angeles. Although I fooled myself into thinking I would wear these clothes, I never did. Yet, I was unable to part with them for several more years. It took a lot of therapy before I was finally able to donate them to a thrift shop.

The separation anxiety I felt when my mom died goes back to losing my dad, who died while I was away at college. My mom also died when I was away on a short trip. When I was on my honeymoon at age 20, a 41-year-old cousin died suddenly, and while I was living in a distant town a year later, a 42-year-old uncle died suddenly. The result was a desire to keep close all those I love in the belief that would keep everyone safe and well. I felt a great amount of anxiety and fear when I was not nearby. I, therefore, had great difficulty when I traveled far from home. I held everyone I love too closely and became hypervigilant, wanting my family to stay healthy and be safe. When saying "goodbye," I tend to linger much too long.

When a loved one passes away, one is aware life will never be the same, though not sure how it will change. One knows it will be different, and feels frightened, confused, hurt, abandoned, lost, alone, and perhaps even guilty. There is a loss of innocence, loss of faith, and a belief life is not fair. Life is forever altered, and there is no going back. The death of a parent equals a sustained kick in the gut. It has been described as "the loss that is forever." Therapists have treated people in their 50s and 60s who lost a parent in early childhood, who still carry the burden of belief that they did something to cause the death. The child often feels responsible for the parent's death.

Regardless of the age of a child when such a loss occurs, shame enters into the child's feelings. At younger ages, they believe they were bad and they were somehow responsible for the loss. At all ages, the shame comes from feeling different from other children. This feeling of difference gets experienced repeatedly through the childhood and adolescent years. People who experience shame feel frozen in the moment. They feel cut off from humankind. When one feels shame or has a shame response, we observe them: Avert their eyes, lower their head, flush, or go pale. Behaviors that express shame occur when: (1) one is withdrawn – the shame becomes internalized and the behavior is moderated, (2) one shows a narcissistic front such as bragging about a car or an achievement, (3) one attacks another with insults, (4) one puts himself down, or (5) one abuses drugs, alcohol, or food. These are all ways people attempt to cover up or blot out the shame. Anything one does to reduce the self-esteem of oneself or another is about shame.

Orphans

In _Dr. Death_, a novel by Jonathan Kellerman, there was the description of a college freshman who lost his mother when she was in her early 40s. While in an angry rage, he says, "My mother came to a horrible end; I'm entitled to be obnoxious. Her death bought me leeway."

The therapist in the novel reports he also lost his father when he was the same age (18) and his mother when he was a few years older. He says he had been very close to his mother, and her loss was profound. He says he felt like he was an orphan. He felt incredibly alone. His father's death was a big blow to his sense of trust. The fact that someone can be taken away from you just like that creates a sense of powerlessness. From that point on, you view the world differently. When one has lost a parent, one tends to hesitate in forming a close relationship. There is the fear that if you care deeply about someone, that person will die. Feelings and memories of a significant loss continue to resurface again and again. There are waves of sadness, which come often at unexpected times.

After trauma or loss, a person can feel that the different parts of his personality are no longer available to him. Emotions of shock, terror, rage, confusion and even pleasure all go scurrying into different parts of their psychic world. This is a creative way to protect the self from re-experiencing the horror over and over. The person is left with parts of himself that cannot be felt. Then, with professional help, he must search for wholeness and a reconnection to his unknown and unfelt parts. One tends to seek wholeness in life.

No one plans to become parentless, and no one, regardless of age, is ready to lose a parent. It can take years for the grieving process and relief to occur. Even adults describe their parents as the center of the nuclear and extended family, as the glue that kept them all together, that provided them with a common interest or a common bond. Although all grown up, one is suddenly "nobody's child." Even when older people have lost their parents, many still report, it is always too soon. These adults say they are now orphans when their last parent dies. While in her therapy with me, Mary, an 80-year-old woman, grieves the loss of her 101-year-old mother and wonders if she did enough to help keep her alive. Mary, too, reported she had now become an orphan.

No matter how many decades pass, no matter how healed, a person still misses that parent, regrets missed opportunities to express feelings, to spend more quality time, to handle certain situations better or to show more appreciation, or to say goodbye. Most adults, even into their own middle or later years, say that on some level, they still feel like the "fatherless" or "motherless child," an "orphan." Often one believes that if you don't have parents, you don't have love now or won't have it in the future. This could be a life-fulfilling prophecy. A deep sense of injustice is felt.

Sara, a 40-year-old woman, was 13 when her 42-year-old mother died. Shocked and frightened, she became fearful of being alone. She cried frequently, became depressed, did poorly in school and gained a lot of weight. She became clumsy and lost whatever self-esteem she had previously had. She became a loner and spent most of her time reading to escape into a safe place. She put her mother on a pedestal and saw her as perfect. She was angry when her father remarried. She felt this was a betrayal of her mother. Her stepmother could never live up to her unrealistic ideal mother image.

When Sara married young and had a child, she missed her mother even more after the baby was born. She regrets not knowing what being a mom was like for her mother and deeply regrets not being able to share her child with her. She wishes she and her mother could have been "moms together."

When Sara's father died when she was 25, she says she felt "orphaned." She felt she lost family history. In order to heal, she worked very hard in therapy. She went back to school, became a nurse, and works with issues of death and dying. Her goal is to help others deal with loss. She has become the family historian and enjoys planning family reunions and celebrating holidays with family members. Sara feels good about establishing family traditions. She feels she is more sensitive now to the needs of others, and she is more able to reach out and say loving things. She does not wait until tomorrow. Sara so clearly remembers going to school one day and never seeing her mother again. She knows 42 will be a difficult year and looks forward to being 43. She fears her own sudden death, leaving her own children without a mother.

Joan, a 28-year-old woman, lost both of her parents in an accident when she was 13. Her father was 43 and mother was 41. Their car was hit by a 16-year-old. Joan, at 16, got her driver's license and had three car accidents and then felt unable to drive for many years. After her parents' deaths, she had to move in with relatives and change schools, thus losing her friends. She became forgetful and unable to concentrate and still has a poor memory. She became shy, quiet, and studious.

Joan reports seeing ghosts of her parents and believed her parents were watching over and taking care of her. She still thinks about them and cries private tears. She never talks about her parents and keeps her feelings to herself. She always felt different and felt no one could ever understand what she went through or what it was like to suffer such a loss. She hopes to someday have a happy marriage like her parents. She believes that when she dies, she will be reunited with her parents.

Abigail, in her 20s, spoke about losing both parents, feeling she was orphaned and feeling she no longer had a home. She believed she was damaged and that damaged people continue to be damaged. Abigail believes "one remains a child until both parents are gone." She reports that she feels a deep sadness and an ache inside when visiting homes of family from her parents' generation. When Abigail sees photographs of children and grandchildren, it hits her: "I am not on anyone's refrigerator door."

Many young people express anger at their parents for having an unhealthy or risky lifestyle and believe their deaths were a result of these behaviors. These young people express hope that they will be able to learn from their parents' behaviors, and that they will be better able to take good care of themselves and stay in good health. They often fear future loss and fear being hurt like that again. They dread holiday times, which are not so enjoyable for those who have lost their parents. They say they begin to feel dread weeks before the holiday season. Although they have their own children, these people say they still feel like "orphans" because they have no parents to visit and no grandparents for their children.

Reflections

For those who have lost both parents, regardless of their age when the second parent dies, the prevailing sentiment is "now we are orphans." It is common in loss of both parents to hear how the losses are "a whole other lifetime away and at the same time, it's only yesterday." The awful moments are played back as if it were yesterday and one's life gets divided between before and after. One is then defined by the loss and often only able to see what was not there or now is there only because of the loss.

When there is early loss of both parents, there is the need to control fears and anxiety about the loss of children, spouse, or animals, and one is always chillingly aware these could be lost at any moment. If our early attachments were broken due to loss of parents, one's adult relationships could include fears of rejection or abandonment. Some might hang onto impaired relationships even when they become toxic. One might expect to be betrayed, disappointed or hurt and therefore, behave in ways that bring about what is most feared. This becomes a self-fulfilling prophecy. Further pain is caused by having fantasies of endless nurturing to make up for this early loss.

One feels anger when the father shows betrayal to the deceased mother by remarrying and giving the mother's belongings to his new wife. The stepmother can never live up to the unrealistic ideal mother image. If the father is not emotionally present or has also passed away, he is not there to provide feelings of autonomy, individuation and a sense of "other-than-mother" experience of the larger world outside the home. If he is not available to provide a role model for healthy masculinity to both son and daughter, or to confirm his daughter's femininity, adult relationships can be deeply impacted. Many women suffer "father hunger" and search for their father in their mates. This can lead to impaired adult relationships. Early parent loss affects both women and men in their choice of mates and influences their relationships, their career choices and their future success in love and work. Often there is a subconscious fear or a hesitancy to surpass the levels reached by the parents.

Girls who need to care for younger siblings, cook, clean the house, shop for food, etc. because their mother has died, are seen as "the little mother or little homemaker." This can also happen if their father was first to die and their mother had to be away at work all day. These young girls are heavily burdened, and sometimes the ill effects are not seen for decades. These effects could present as resentment toward their husbands and children. Often their resentment surfaces by their refusal to care for their own children or their own homes. Frequently, when a father dies first, the son is left to become "the man of the house," which is also too much of a burden. Sometimes the son is left with a depressed and needy mother to care for, which also has its lingering and often damaging effects on his future choice of mate and his lack of healthy relationship role-modeling.

Often, the youngest children feel invisible after the loss of a parent. They believe their inner pain was not seen or acknowledged by anyone. The resulting loneliness can lead to chronic grief. They are left with the feeling that no one was there for them and no one can take the parent's place. Regarding the second death, whether anticipated or unexpected, many still feel caught off guard. No one is ready to go through that sadness, grief or pain again. To experience those feelings and to see the world again through a veil or shield is almost unbearable to many. When one becomes an orphan, one has a new realization of one's own mortality. There is a deep knowing in every cell of our being that we are the ones who are next in line and many hope that their parents will be waiting on the other side.

Some say they were only able to endure the second parent loss because they were then grown, had their own spouse, significant other and/ or their own children. One's newly formed family provides emotional support and a healing of the emptiness and loss. The financial struggles can be relieved and perhaps one can even regain self-development through the symbolic recreation of the "good parent." Sometimes, however, too much of a burden is placed on the spouse or partner by being expected to take on the role of a 'good parent', which is often more than one is able to provide. Without intervention, there can be too much stress put on the relationship. Often the person who suffers early parent loss places blame on these losses for having married too young, having difficult relationships, not going to college, not pursuing a career, having low self-esteem, and being unhappy.

CHAPTER 5
Going Forward

After the death of the first parent, and then after subsequent losses, those who survive must still live on. They begin the rest of their lives by going forward. This occurs whether the grieving person wants to go forward or not, as life does not stop. Life and time continue, and one moves forward too. Learning how one will survive begins on day one.

Each new day begins without the parent who is loved, remembered, and missed. The entire first year after the loss brings new firsts: the first birthday, Christmas and other holidays, Father's Day, Mother's Day, and family milestones without the loved one. They will all be noted and marked as days and events no longer celebrated with the deceased. In time, hopefully, each person will be able to come to terms with this loss and create ways to adjust to this new "normal" and go forward into their future. These new rituals and new beginnings are part of the process of remembering, honoring, and slowly healing.

Anniversary Times

Anniversary dates often bring foreboding and fearfulness of one's own death. The parents' passing is an important initiating life passage. When parents are gone, we are the next generation to be the adults, to make decisions, to give advice and to be the role models. We face our own mortality, we "get it" – we are "next in line." We look at the fragility of life. We know if someone who had been there is now suddenly not there, we wonder who else can be taken away. We have to live with this incredible fragility, being made worse because our buffers (parents) are now gone.

The anniversaries bring up pictures, memories and old feelings causing one to become more emotional, depressed or unsettled. It often takes years to really understand that the person with whom one has been since birth will never be seen again. This produces a pain that ebbs and flows through the rest of one's life, sometimes in a quiet secret silent place and sometimes right out front.

Therapists believe "holiday blues" or "holiday depression" is connected to anniversary reactions, such as delayed feelings of grief over past losses not adequately mourned. The anniversary of a death often reminds one of the person who died when this anniversary and memory coincides with a joyful time, such as a holiday or a birth or other family milestone event. The person might experience guilt or shame along with the sadness. This causes one to experience or express sadness in the face of a joyful event, and often people are in tears at happy lifecycle events. One tends to mark anniversary times with an emotional response.

Some anniversary reactions seen are a mom becoming ill when her daughter turns the same age she had been when her own mother became ill and subsequently died. In this type of situation, the mom feels as she did when she was the child and also as her own mom felt as the parent. This will again bring up all the long-ago buried emotions, especially debilitating fears. Most fears include fear of anything happening to them or to their children and spouses. There is a belief system, based on observations, that similar experiences such as illness and often death occur at the same age in families over several generations. An emotional patterning occurs and expectations are set up. If one expects to become ill at a certain age, it often happens that way.

People tend to see themselves in others and connect with the pain and sadness they can instinctively pick up on. Greta, a woman who lost her own mother when she was in fifth grade, learned of a boy in her son's fifth grade class who lost his mother at the same age as she was. Greta says she searches for him in the class photo as if "I am looking for myself. I search for his/my face and his/my sadness and pain."

When a loss occurs at any stage of a child's development, the child tends to regress back to an earlier stage when life was happier. Sometimes, a person gets stuck in this regressed phase and has trouble moving on to continue normal development. Marty, a 30-year-old man had the look of the 13-year-old boy that he was when he had lost his second parent. His demeanor was immature, as was the look on his face, as if time was stopped when he was just 13. He is like a 13-year-old boy stuck in a 30-year-old body. If not adequately helped, the child remains, to a significant degree, the child he was at that phase and age when the loss was sustained and the child becomes developmentally stunted.

When one has passed the age of the parents' death, there is usually a feeling of gratitude. It is both a gift, and also a strange realization that one has lived beyond the age of the parent, especially in the loss of the same-sex parent. Often the feelings of sadness and loneliness connect one to the lost parent, and one even connects to others through common sadness.

Paula, a 35-year-old woman, described how as a young teenager she left the house after an argument with her widowed mother, and her mother passed away while she was out. Paula blamed herself: "If I were home, this would not have happened, I would have saved her." She felt abandoned, alone, guilt-ridden and fearful of the future. She had to live with relatives. Paula often had dreams that her parents came back. She would feel happy about their return, and suddenly they would be yanked away again as she tried to hold on to them. Paula then felt abandoned over and over again. She dreaded the anniversary of that day for all the years that followed. After a lot of professional help in her 20s, Paula was able to regard herself as a survivor and felt more mature. She now has her own family and keeps everyone close together. She talks about carrying her parents inside, which provides a great degree of comfort. Special milestones and anniversary times are still very difficult. Ultimately, she says, she has "a protective shell" around her. Paula now believes she is strong enough to deal with whatever life brings.

The impressionable child believes the parent's death was due to their inner wishes, their spoken anger, or to a particular behavior they did or failed to do. This belief can affect one's life throughout adulthood unless there is skilled intervention. Maggie, a 30-year-old woman, tells of how her mother, a 35-year-old single mom, left home for an evening out. Maggie was in her young teen years and didn't want her mother to go out. She shouted at her mother, "Don't leave, I hate you, I wish you were dead." Her mother was killed in a car accident that night and Maggie's wish came true. She then had to live with an elderly grandmother and her life-long guilt. All too often these are the last words a child speaks or the last wishes in one's head before a tragic event occurs, and it appears the wish came true. Maggie reported how she felt responsible for her mother's death and how she became hypervigilant about her grandmother's well being. Her main focus was on keeping her grandmother alive. She dreamed about her mother and always wondered what would have happened if she did not make that wish, if her mother had lived, and if her mother could have forgiven her. Maggie says she always wished she could go back to the day before her ugly wish. She could not imagine life beyond age 35 and felt she didn't know how to live. She imagines dying at 35 and saying, "See, I told you I would die." Maggie eventually received a lot of help and developed a healthier and more trusting outlook on life. She was able to create some special rituals to remember and honor her mother.

Leslie, a 50-year-old woman, talks about being 20 and losing both parents on the same day. Her mom died of a long illness and her dad had a heart attack and died instantly. There was a double funeral. After 20 years, Leslie began to come to terms with her parents' loss. She talks about anniversary times being very sad and she misses her parents at lifecycle events. She believes her parents are watching over her and her children. Leslie asks them for guidance and strength. Also, at times of accomplishment, she thinks: "Thank you, Mom, thank you, Dad." She sees them as her Guardian Angels. She feels herself thinking, "We made it Mom, Dad." Leslie feels their spirits all around her. She is thus able to incorporate her parents into her daily life.

Josh, a 29-year-old man, lost both his parents within four years – his mother when he was 14 and his father at 18. His father's death was sudden, and he was devastated. Josh had barely begun to cope with his mother's death following a long illness. He was angry and felt alone amid family and friends who rallied to provide emotional support. For many years, Josh felt envy at those who had both their parents, who took family vacations, and had an extended-family life. As a senior in high school, Josh lost interest in his studies and did not attend his graduation. He was not able to go away to college as had been his plan. He eventually received an education while commuting to a local college. Josh felt responsible for his younger brother, and was fearful of leaving him alone, even though they lived with friends. Today they are both very supportive of each other.

Josh says he feels a huge void, an emptiness that continues. He says that "something is missing," and he believes others can't understand how he feels. He has dreams of both parents being together. This provides a bit of comfort. Holiday and anniversary times and milestone events are the most difficult. He always wishes his parents were still alive and fantasizes they are able to see him and his brother and that somehow his parents are aware of how they are doing. Josh often wonders how life would have been different had one or both of his parents lived. He is aware life is finite and fragile. He expressed, "Life can come to a screeching halt without preparation or warning and no one has any control over that." Today, he struggles with his own health risks. Josh is doing his best to move toward a healthier lifestyle. He believes his parents became ill because they didn't take good enough care of themselves. Josh gets angry at himself when he continues to smoke, eat poorly, and doesn't exercise. His goal is to live in ways that would make his parents proud.

Bart, a 35-year-old man, spoke about losing both parents before he was 20. He felt lost, alone, and insecure. He went from dependent to independent in a moment. His strongest ties to his parents and the most enjoyable times as a family centered around food and eating. His mother was a wonderful cook, and she prepared the holiday meals for their extended family. Bart's quiet, gentle, warm nature seems to reflect that of his mother. To this day, he still enjoys eating the foods which remind him of her and of their family meals. Bart uses food to remember his parents at anniversary times, but this also causes him concern about his own health, since he is overweight and depressed. He feels he swallows down his repressed emotions, seeking comfort through food, which comes but is short-lived.

Visiting Graves

Visiting graves of one's parents can be a healing experience. This is a ritual often described as a source of comfort. Many people visit the cemetery and talk directly to their loved ones. The unit has been broken, but going to the graves helps us to reconnect.

There is a remark that my sister and I have made in jest, yet there is much truth to it. We say, "Let's go home and visit our parents." What we mean is that we will travel to our hometown and we will go to the cemetery and visit our parents' graves. There is comfort in knowing our loved ones are there behind the tombstones. We put small stones on each of their gravestones to let them know we are there. The placement of these smaller stones lets our loved ones know they are still loved, missed, thought about and visited.

We take comfort each time by seeing the religious symbolism and lettering on each tombstone. We again read their names, dates of birth and death and who they were: Beloved Husband/Wife, Mother/Father, Grandparent, Son of/ Daughter of, Brother/Sister. We note their ages and again see ourselves as having lived past both their ages. We note the passing of time and see our place in relationship to them and see where we are along our own path in our own journey, still a part of them and yet separate, moving forward. Somehow, although we are nostalgic, maybe tearful, we always leave with a sense of being unburdened, of feeling positive spirit energy – coming from them – coming from us – coming from the fact that we visited and reconnected – that we let them know they continue to be a part of us and our lives as we bravely go forward without them.

Our religious tradition is to put the small stones onto the permanent marked gravestones but other traditions include planting small trees or flowers on the graves. Some people have the ritual of visiting at all anniversary dates, holidays or perhaps annually. Sometimes it's a visit that includes extended family members or a spouse or one's children or other significant people in one's life. Other times it is a solitary visit one makes for a wide variety of personal needs.

Reflections

When we go on with our journey, we might have the thought, "How can we live adequately without our parents?" Or we might think, "We must go on and live for our parents to make up for what they missed and also to make them proud of us." Finally, hopefully, we will survive our losses by having our own wonderful family – our own loving and supportive spouse, and our own precious children and grandchildren. Visiting graves and establishing rituals to help heal wounds of loss will continue as they are woven into the fabric of our lives, enabling us to heal and go forward.

CHAPTER 6

Impact of Parental Loss on the Next Generation

Just like a tree is as strong as its long, sturdy roots with its graceful branches and lush healthy leaves, we are only as strong as our roots (our heritage) and our branches (our offspring) with their leaves (our grandchildren). Just as the tree passes on its nourishment to its saplings, we pass on our current understanding to our children, who are our present and to our grandchildren who are our future and our immortality. What we pass on from our own heritage helps nourish them, gives them richness, depth, and strength. We are all the sum total of those who came before us. Our wholeness and ideal self is composed of our own spirituality, which is fed by the wisdom of our heritage, our personal ancestors, and the group, community, culture, and belief systems of which we are a part.

Our older generations have known the lives of several generations of family. They have experienced enough life to know how quickly time passes and how important each being is. They can live on from generation to generation through those who are young and willing to pass along their wisdom, their life stories and their names to each new generation. The older generation then becomes a part of each new generation; their good deeds, their characters, and their names are honored and passed along.

Through our own study of ourselves and the knowledge of our culture, tradition, and heritage we are able to connect to our inner spirits, our soul, or our best or most ideal self. We learn about our own spirituality or our own godliness through personal awareness or mindfulness, meditation, and other such modalities. Our own personal identity is built by filling in our foundation, reaching down into our roots and then building on that by including our own unique needs and experiences, which we then pass on to our own future generations which bring our immortality.

Wounds

Wounds also get passed down from generation to generation. The experiences of each generation become the legacy of future generations of children and grandchildren. Our parents' wounds that have not been healed are passed on as such. They become a part of who we are. We carry them as "badges of honor" or as "burdens." They become our baggage that we carry with us, adding to it and only parting with it when we are forced to, when it causes us emotional or physical harm.

Memories of early parent loss can come through the body. The body remembers what the mind can repress. This can lead to physical illness even through adulthood. When a parent dies, you lose a past. The pain remains as a way to maintain loyalty to the loved parent and to keep the memory of the loved one alive. One often fears that the loss of the wound will diminish the memory and make the parent disappear.

The effects of unresolved grief can and do last into the next generation. Since both my father and I were struck by early parent loss, I always felt hooked into his own unresolved pain, and the thread continued with his death and became the legacy I fear I have passed on. My father's pain, loss, disappointment, and resentment for his own mother's death, as well as other life circumstances and their lingering effects, were strongly felt in me, his eldest child, who was most attuned to him. His over protective nature, his ever-watchful eyes, his strong regard for ritual, and the very high value he placed on the "mother-role," as well as his lack of being mothered were all transmitted to me. I was in tune with his emotions to such an extent that I carried them inside me and made them my own. With my own traumatic event, the loss of him, I added my own emotional wound onto the already deep pile that was his. The burden of this heaviness has added to my life struggle. Through the years of my own individual therapy, my training as a psychotherapist, and my own personal growth, I have been able to reduce the load to a more manageable size.

The wounds of our parents helped shape them and affected the ways they lived, loved, and parented. We absorbed them as they shaped us, and eventually passed them onto our own children. My father lost his 20-year-old mother during a pogrom in the streets of the Ukraine. I was aware from my earliest consciousness of my father's loss, sadness, and burden of his ongoing unresolved emotions. His influence on me, which came from a wounded place, was very strong. As one grows to adulthood, there is often the awareness that one's own fears of loss, death, illness, and safety issues will get passed on to the next generation. The next generation absorbs the unspoken fears and anxiety and makes them their own. Often these children grow up to feel they had been smothered or overprotected, often held onto too tightly and the parent cannot let go.

Worries

I, and other moms whom I have interviewed, share the same experience – we all agree that when a mom has lost a parent during her childhood or adolescence, she passes on her fears and intense worry about health and safety issues to her children. The worry is usually too intense and too much and the children are unable to absorb it all. Because she knows from such a young age that death is possible, the mom worries and watches her children too closely. She says: "If I watch them, they will be safe and healthy." Yet, to her, the unthinkable is not only possible, but all too real. She knows this feared road has already been traveled, and it can happen again. So, her eyes and arms watch and grip and hold on for dear life. "If I am there and ever watchful, they will be safe and well." Yet, even as we watch and hold on, we know we can never make them or ourselves safe enough and we can never bargain enough. We have no control; no one and nothing can save them or us. The unthinkable is the "stranger" and the "evil eye" is ever present, lurking around every corner, and one must be ever vigilant.

When my youngest son was two months old, our good friends lost their infant son. I became distraught and immobile – unable to handle this new possibility of loss (the loss of a child) or to allow it to enter my protective space. I spent days clinging to my baby as I sat in my rocking chair. My heart ached for them. For many days I cried for their sadness and was unable to move beyond my rocking chair or let go of my baby, lest evil would befall him. Even today, my innermost nature and tendency is to hold on and resist change. I tend to want to hold onto my family and friends. I save old junk because of sentiment, and I have trouble dealing with the pain of letting go when the time comes to move on, even when it is clear a relationship or situation no longer works. I move reluctantly, even when I know it could be pleasurable to make a change.

Ruth, aged 26, reports that her mother lost her own 52-year-old mother when she was 22, just three months before her wedding. She had always known her mother was angry and sad that her own mother was not at her wedding or there when her children were born. She describes how her mother "built a wall around herself to keep out the pain of loss and grief, but it also kept out her children and husband." The entire family felt unable to penetrate this wall. Ruth grew up feeling worried that it was her fault that her mother was so distant. She feels she missed a lot by not having closeness with her mother, who was never able to show much affection or say "I love you." She knew she was loved, but would have enjoyed hearing it.

Ruth recalls that her mother was always afraid something would happen to her children, and as a result became too strict, overprotective and controlling. She remembers her mother often saying: "If only your grandmother were alive, you'd be so close," or "If only my mother were here to enjoy my children (her grandchildren)." As a result, Ruth felt she never was able to bring her mother pleasure. She never had her mother as a whole person. She grew up feeling burdened by her mother's sadness and emotional heaviness. Ruth feels she continues to carry this burden and that her own children have also been affected.

Nathan, a 31-year-old man, reports that his mother lost both her mother and father while she was a teenager. Her whole life revolved around her husband and sons, creating a suffocating environment. She was worried most of the time, fearful, emotional, and overly sensitive, while also being dominant and controlling. She became overly anxious when there was a lack of order. She instilled guilt in her sons by putting an end to all communication about their feelings by saying "you are lucky you have your parents." Although Nathan knew his mom was proud of him, she was unable to express her feelings or give compliments to him or his brothers.

There is often a great sense of worry that one will become ill with the same or similar symptoms as his parent experienced prior to death when his own child reaches the age he was when his parent died. Studies have shown that this does in fact happen. A parent dies at a certain age and his adult child experiences the same or similar illness at that same age. One sees himself in his child and has the strong fear that history will repeat itself. The feeling self that has been repressed often comes to the surface when the child reminds the parent of that time and those feelings, and that time coincides with the same age when the parent was deceased. There is some literature to support the observations that people do become ill or die at some predetermined meaningful time. For example, a 28-year-old woman lost her husband. She had a premonition she would be a widow at that age because her mother, grandmother, and great grandmother were all widowed at that age. Specific anniversaries, ages, or dates have become emotionally-invested deadlines, which have specific meaning to a person. Many people see certain dates as their destiny and believe they will be spared until then, and often this premonition becomes reality.

Ben, a 35-year-old man, lost his father at age 40; his father (Ben's grandfather) died at 42. As Ben grows older, he fears reaching 40. He has the fantasy that he too will die young like his father and grandfather. He attempts to take good care of himself physically and emotionally. He believes he is healthier than his father was. He feels he is less driven than his father. He has a more moderate temperament and is more easygoing. Ben is a teacher as his father was. Ben attempts to live his life to the fullest, enjoying his wife and child. He is an involved father, developing a close and meaningful relationship with his child. As he approaches age 40, he realizes how very young his father and grandfather were and how much life they missed. Ben works hard at being upbeat and happy, and tries to help others to be happy.

Eva, a 60-year-old woman, reports that she lost her 25-year-old mother to cancer when she was three years old. Her mother, at age 5, lost her own mother at age 25. Eva's father, unable to care for her, put her into foster care. Her trust in people and life disappeared. She became a person who worries a lot. When she turned 25, she had a horrible year. Eva was physically and emotionally ill that entire year. Since she was married and had a child, she worried that she would die and leave her own family. Eva says that somehow she was able to get through that difficult time. She reports having had "no role models for life, knowing only what was in stories and books." Today, Eva feels proud of herself that she was able to raise her family and enjoy her grandchildren. If her mother had lived, she believes she would have been a totally different person. She would have achieved success in a career and would have been more trusting of others. Eva believes she would have had a better sense of self and a stronger self worth. She never heard anyone say she was "beautiful" or "special." She does believe that her husband, upon whom she has been very dependent, has been there for her as a "good parent," which she never had as a child. Eva tends to stay aloof from people, is fearful of too much closeness, and still has some "trust issues." She keeps a journal and fears living to "an old age." She also worries about outliving her husband. She fears she has passed on her emotional stress to her children. She also worries about people being angry at her and tends to maintain relationships long past their end point. It is difficult for Eva to face endings.

Adam, a young man of 32, was 10 years old when he lost his 45-year-old father. His paternal grandfather was also very young when he died. Since his father suffered the loss of his own father at such a young age, he became a worrier, and he lived with a sense of urgency, trying to accomplish a lot in a short time. At age 10, when Adam lost his own father, he reports that he felt as if "someone flicked a switch and I will now go down a different path throughout my life." Adam went to the funeral, but not the cemetery. He says he has never been able to go there. His family never spoke of his father, yet he was aware of his mother's grief, and he felt saddened by her upset. Adam felt he had to grow up faster and become the man of the house. He felt protective of his mother. Adam recalls that he cherished his father's possessions and wanted to grow up to be like him. As he went through school, he felt self-conscious about not having a father and kept it a secret. He spoke of having dreams and fantasies that his father was not really dead. He dreamed that his father was taken away, but he would come back. Adam became a person who worries a lot and always felt his father's death was too final. He feels a melancholy presence, especially at happy events. There is always a worried, nagging feeling that something is missing.

Reflections

The child who lost his or her same-sex parent often experiences the emotionally-invested markers of the age he or she was at the time of the traumatic event, the age of the parent, the exact day, date, month and year. This stressful time may lie dormant until the individual has a child who is the same age as when his own earlier trauma occurred. At this time, symptoms, illness or even death can occur. Psychosis, coronary heart disease, hypertension, colitis, arthritis, depression or anxiety are the physical manifestations of trauma that have been observed. Anniversary emotional patterning and the importance of psychogenic stress is undeniable.

For women who lost both a father and a husband, the eldest son often takes on the role of "my mother's father" and/or "my mother's husband." The mother weaves glorious fantasies about her own father and the boy's father (her husband), and believes life would have been so different if only he/they had lived. Happiness and life's perfection was the strong, smart capable father who could teach all about the world and the meaning of life. Growing up fatherless left these sons to become fatherless fathers. There was then often a glorified fantasy of the paternal role and very little reality. Men raised without fathers often become amateur parents and might even be amateur human beings. Many people who suffer parent loss as the first generation or the second often believe their lives would have been different had the parent lived. They would have been spared pain and suffering. They would have had support and guidance, would have had an education or a better education and surely a more financially successful or secure future.

There is a profound sense of loss and sadness when children are deprived of their grandparents (and of course, a profound sense of loss and sadness for the grandparent who left before having the opportunity to enjoy and love their grandchildren). Grandparents typically provide praise, unconditional love, family history, holiday gatherings and presents for no reason. Bereavement is a consequence of the loss of someone sigfnificant.

CHAPTER 7
Creative Outcomes

"Like all traumas, being orphaned may, at times, become the basis of personality strengths. Character traits of stoicism, ambition and generativity can be intensified. Diminished fear of death, in some adults with childhood parental loss, can result in remarkable acts of courage and sacrifice." (Salman Akhtar, MD, 2011 – *Matters of Life and Death*, p.163)

"The presence of 'God-given' talents (artistic inclination) and superior intelligence can greatly modify the impact of being orphaned. A healthy and ambitious nucleus of personality can be organized around such extraordinary abilities and lead to great fame and social success. The positive traits of courage, resilience, imaginativeness and creativity displayed by these individuals might have been fueled by the trauma of childhood parental loss." (Salman Akhtar, MD, 2011 – *Matters of Life and Death*, p. 163)

The trauma of parental loss imposes pressure on the psyche to create whatever is necessary to resolve issues of frustration, identity and feelings of emptiness. Some seek a sense of personal power or attempt to avenge a bad destiny or compensate in some way for the loss. Some of these people have become famous scholars, performers, statesmen, politicians, poets, artists and even very dangerous people who committed crime. Some have done great acts of kindness and have given much good to society. Others have done the most evil acts on humanity that one can ever imagine.

Famous People Who Lost a Parent as a Child, Adolescent or Young Adult

These famous people include prophets, philosophers, kings, musicians, singers, writers, poets, political leaders and film personalities. They include the following:

At 10 months, Albert Camus, a writer, lost his 29-year-old father. Camus wrote _The First Man_ in 1960, a psychological journey to explore his roots, and a quest for the father he never knew. He despaired at not knowing about his father or his father's life. Camus died in a car accident at age 46.

At 15 months, John Paul Sartre, a writer, lost his father. He was raised by his mother and grandparents.

At 15 months, Barbra Streisand, writer, actress, singer, producer and director, lost her 35-year-old father. She wrote "Yentl" as a dedication to her father's memory and his inspiration in her life.

At 2 years, Harold Brodsky, a staff writer at <u>The New Yorker</u>, lost his mother.

At 3 years, Mariska Hargitay, an actress, lost her mother, Jane Mansfield, in a car accident. She says she had a "late start in life. I had no follow-through and didn't think I was very good." She married late and had her child late – at age 42. She says if her mother had lived, she "would have been more on time."

At 5 years, Madonna, actress and singer, lost her mother.

At 5 years, Bernice King, writer, lost her father, Martin Luther King, assassinated in 1968. She speaks of a large void and a sense of emptiness. She tries to connect with him spiritually. She finds his resemblances in the mirror in the shape of her eyes and the cut of her chin. She, too, became a minister (reverend) and the cadence of her preaching style resembles his. She wrote a book that strikes at the heart, encouraging the restoration of family, community and obligation.

At 5 years, Dylan McDermott, actor, lost his mother.

At 6 years, Justin Simpson, child of O.J. Simpson, lost his mother, Nicole Brown Simpson.

At 6 years, C.S. Lewis, writer and poet, lost his mother.

At 7 years, Mary Gordon, writer, essayist, lost her father. She always thought this was the most important thing people could know about her. She says she has remained devoted to his memory. "He hovers in the margins of all my writings."

At 7 years, Jennifer Landon, actress, lost her 54-year-old father, Michael Landon.

At 8 years, Geraldine Ferraro, first female vice presidential candidate, lost her father.

At 8 years, Sylvia Plath, writer and poet, lost her father. She wrote a poem: "Daddy." It focused on her feelings for her father.

At 9 years, Sydney Simpson, daughter of O.J. Simpson, lost her mother, Nicole Brown Simpson.

At 9 years, Julia Roberts, actress, lost her father.

At 9 years, Merle Haggard, musician and singer, lost his father.

At 10 years, Peter Fonda, actor, lost his mother.

At 11 years, Rosie O'Donnell, actress, comedian, talk show host, lost her mother.

At 12 years, Jessica Savitch, TV anchor and journalist, lost her 33-year-old father. She died in a car accident at age 36.

At 12 years, James Woods, writer and actor, lost his father.

At 12 years, Virginia Woolf, writer, lost her mother.

At 13 years, Alfred Dupont, benefactor for children's health care, lost both parents.

At 13 years, Jane Fonda, actress, lost her mother.

At 13 years, Les Brown, writer, motivational speaker, lost his mother.

At 13 years, Amy Tan, writer, lost her father.

At 14 years, Larry Kane, writer, newscaster, journalist, lost his mother.

At 15 years, Billy Crystal, actor and writer, lost his father. His book and Broadway show, _700 Sundays_, was autobiographical and dedicated to the memory of his father.

At 17 years, Jan Kerouac, writer and singer, lost her father, Jack Kerouac. Her story is told in _Train Song_ – dedicated to her father's memory.

At 19 years, T. Berry Brazelton, expert on child development, a professor of pediatrics and psychiatry, pediatrician and writer, lost his 49-year-old father.

At 19 years, Mandy Patinkin, writer, actor, singer and performer, lost his father.

At 24 years, Ellen Goodman, writer, lost her father.

Stories and Quotes from Famous People

Prince Albert of Monaco, son of Princess Grace Kelly and Prince Rainier III of Monaco, says it took him 25 years to be able to deal with the loss of his mother, a Philadelphia born actress. She died suddenly, at age 52, in a car accident. His siblings, Stephanie and Caroline, were teenagers at the time, and Albert was in his early 20s.

Albert finally felt ready to showcase her legacy in Tokyo in 2007. He displayed hundreds of objects, such as her letters and clothing. His intention was to celebrate her life and to keep her memory alive for the next generation. He reported he had a special relationship with her. She always told him he had good, strong instincts and he should follow them. He describes this event in Tokyo as an emotional but joyful process. Albert also reported that his sisters, Stephanie and Caroline, had lost their bearing when their mother died, which caused them to have difficulty establishing and maintaining relationships and intimacy.

Art Buchwald, who died at age 81, lost his mother when he was three. His father was unable to care for him and he was sent to an orphanage until he joined the Marines during World War II when he was 17. He had survived much adversity, yet he was very successful. He was a political columnist, a writer and a celebrity.

Adele Aron Greenspun, photo journalist and writer, says her book _Daddies_ is to honor fathers everywhere. She succeeded in capturing the "essence of father – the loving, teaching relationships between father and child." She expressed through photography the "nurturing side of men and the pure joy and pleasures of the sweet and nourishing relationship between children and their daddies."

Patti Davis, daughter of Ronald Reagan, calls people on the anniversary dates of their losses to say she remembers and is thinking about them. She says, "These are days like no other." She feels like it's a complicated day of emotions and no one wants to go through those days alone. We tend to measure and define ourselves around that point in time when we lost a special person. We speak of who we were before and who we became after. This redefines us each year. Often, we feel isolated in our emotions until someone listens and says, "Me too."

Patti reports: "I feel my father in every gust of wind and hear him in the movement of leaves as the breeze sweeps through the trees." Patti has shared how "death always feels surprising, even after anticipating it for a while. One can't anticipate the emptiness left behind – in the places once filled by a life. These losses and feelings that come from the pain of missing someone so terribly have to be integrated into our lives." She reminds us that "death is an awkward subject – a language none of us feels fluent in, no matter how much experience we've had." She says, "Anyone who has lost a loved one knows you never move on from missing that person and marking the day he left. We want someone else to remember too, so we're not sitting by that river bank alone."

Patrick Dempsey, at age 42, was interviewed in Parade, April 27, 2008. He told Parade that he was 18 when his father, an insurance salesman, died. He says "that's a big loss. It would have been nice to have been able to communicate with my father as a man – not just a kid. I would like to have had that. But you have to find it in yourself. You have to learn how to be your own father." He spends a lot of quality time with his daughter and infant sons. He remembers when "I would do stuff with my father and my mother. You want those moments. They go by so quickly, so you try to get them in when you can."

Billy Crystal wrote and performed in *700 Sundays*, an autobiographical play memorializing and paying tribute to his father, Jack, who was very important in the world of jazz. His father died at age 53 when Billy was 15. Billy went on to be a performer and comedian, influenced by his father and the world of entertainers that he was exposed to by his father.

Both Dostoevsky and Nietzche lost their fathers in childhood. Both men, from that time on through adulthood, struggled with the idea of God's existence. To have lost God meant madness to Nietzche. His concept that "God is dead" and having a world without a deity drove him insane. Dostoevsky in *The Brothers Karamazov* stated that, "in a godless world, all is permitted." One might say that these two men equated the loss of their fathers with a loss of God, spirit, order or meaning in life.

Dr. Paulina F. Kernberg, child psychiatrist, said: "The trauma from divorce is second only to a parent's death."

Virginia Woolf, writer, who lost her mother at age 12, said: "This is an emotional wound from which I never entirely recovered."

Dylan Thomas in *Collected Poems,* New York – New Directions, 1957, wrote: "After the First Death, there is no other."

Dr. Dan Gottlieb, a psychologist, wrote: "Children grow up in their parents' shadows and, therefore, carry the burden of their parents' unfinished business. The child grows up trying to do what they deep down think will make their parents happy. Mostly, it can never really be done."

Dr. Dan Gottlieb also wrote, "In trying to protect our children from the pains of life, we inadvertently protect them from wonderful lessons, such as courage. Protecting one another from your grief, anger, or fear only creates barriers and makes everyone more lonely and isolated."

Amy Tan, writer, lost her mother at age 13 and said: "When you lose a parent, you spend a lifetime excavating and learning who that person was and who were the people in their life, and how it all relates to you and the whole history of your place in the world. So much of who they were remains a mystery to you." From Inquirer Magazine February, 2001.

Barbra Streisand, famous actress, singer, writer, producer and director, reported in an interview in the L.A. Times calendar section in 1983 that she was 15 months old when her 35-year-old father died. She says she was the only child in her neighborhood without a father and felt different. She said she "grew up always looking for Daddy." Barbra says, "Inspiration comes from your unconscious, your gut, your soul, your very core." Emotionally, Barbra had trouble believing that what she does is "good enough." If she noticed something was good, she would become fearful that "God will take it away." She has said that this is the price paid for the loss of her father.

She created, acted in and directed the critically acclaimed and financially successful film, "Yentl," based on the story by Isaac Bashevis Singer. She says by creating "Yentl," she was able to create a Daddy. The first four words of the story are: "After my father's death," and Barbra says that she was immediately hooked and knew this would be her movie. Her final credit reads: "... this film is dedicated to my father and to all our fathers."

She says, "Yentl has allowed me to come to terms with the memory of my father whom I never knew – it has released me from the ghost of my father so I was able to make him live a little longer." She says her drive to make Yentl came from a visit to her father's grave. On his tombstone is written, "Beloved Teacher and Scholar." He was an intellectual, and received his Ph.D. His dissertation was on Dante and Shakespeare. Like her father, she always had a strong will and accomplished what she wanted to. She reports that like her father, she loves to learn and has a lot of passion. It has been reported that it was this strong will, great passion and determination that got this project (Yentl) developed and produced. This achievement proved to her that one does not need to be a man in order to accomplish important work. Yentl is a story about a woman who learned from her father the subject matter only boys were permitted to learn. She eventually travels to America where she will no longer need to pretend to be the person she already became.

Merle Haggard lost his father when he was nine years old. He felt older than his years and by age 11 felt he was grown and was on his own. He became a troubled teen and acted out against society. He even spent some time in jail. He reports in Parade Magazine, December 2000, that before his father died, he was a good child, but his life on the farm and his good upbringing were interrupted. He says that when he lost his father, his life was "blown to pieces." He was devastated and never got over it. He says that he suffered loneliness throughout his adult life. It took until he was 60, married for the fifth time with two children, to finally find happiness. He realized his family was the most important part of his life. Merle's father played the fiddle, guitar, banjo and mandolin, and had a small hillbilly band. He worked as a carpenter on the Santa Fe Railroad. Merle turned to music as a way to reconnect with his father. Merle's "Sing a Sad Song," was a big hit, one of many in his long career.

Geraldine Ferraro, in an article for the Boston Globe four years after she lost the bid for vice president, looked back at that historic moment.

She discussed the many problems she and her family faced. These included I.R.S. issues, her son's drug addiction, and surviving major surgery. When asked if she had known what was going to happen in these four years, would she have run for vice president? Ms. Ferraro, then 52 years old, said: "The worst experience of my life was when I was 8 years old and I awoke to find my father dying of a heart attack right before my eyes. That's what I compare everything to."

Bernie Siegel, physician and author, says: "If one deals with anger and despair when they first appear, illness need not occur. When we don't deal with our emotional needs, we set ourselves up for physical illness." Dr. Siegel reports that the second year after a loss is even worse than the first. "By the second year, the reality of the loss just sits inside. The permanence has hit. It takes one to a deeper, darker place."

Morrie Schwartz, as told to Mitch Albom in _Tuesdays with Morrie_, says: "Slow down and enjoy life. Learn how to die and you learn how to live. Death ends a life, not a relationship."

T. Berry Brazelton said: "No matter what our age, we all yearn for attention, appreciation, acceptance, approval. The best things parents and grandparents can do for their children and grandchildren are to love them and shower them with unmitigated love – a love where you don't hold anything back or wish things were different."

Randy Pausch, in _The Last Lecture_, shortly before his death from cancer in his late 40s, wrote: "No amount of material things can make up for a missing parent. Children try to figure out what the parent wanted them to become and they might choose fields that are all wrong for them. Parents want their kids to feel they are there with them, supportive of any path chosen."

Jerry, a writer, spoke of his reactions to the loss of his father and his father's influence on him. He recalls a quote by Jung who said: "Nothing has stronger influence on us psychologically than the unlived life of our parents." This young writer says that his father never told him that he wanted to be a writer, but he didn't have to. He says, "Even in a family as given as ours to endless discussion, and endless complaining, the really important feelings were rarely put into words. After all these years, I still can't say how much my need to write has to do with my innermost sense of purpose, my destiny – and how much it has to do with my father. Following the clues is like making my way down a hallway in darkness, my hand following the wall to the deeper darkness within. These sentences, which seem to move across the page so surely, trail ghosts behind them. Are the words really my own? When I tell myself the words aren't good enough – which is my harsh judgment about nearly everything I write – is that my voice or his?"

Saul, a 20-year-old man, lost his father at age 14. His father had been an athlete who played competitively. As a 16-year-old, Saul took up a sport in memory of his father. He always felt his father was his constant companion every time he played his sport.

Morris, a 40-year-old man, lost his father when he was 15. His father had cancer, and Morris became a psychotherapist who works with cancer patients. He wants to help those who are ill and help their families to deal with their losses better than he and his family were able to deal with theirs. Morris says he has a fatalistic dread of becoming ill as his father had. On some level, he believes doing family therapy will create a "magical bargain," and he will be able to "escape fate."

In an article that contained an interview with Yehuda Amichai, he discussed the "Precision of Pain and the Blurriness of Joy." He says, "We tend to generalize joy and memories of good times blur, but we are exquisitely precise when describing emotional pain. We recall every nuance. Everything associated with pain is as clear as the first moment. It is right there again – in an instant. All we need is something to trigger the memory. Therefore, one needs to learn to speak among the pains."

Rabbi Yitzchak Vorst, author of _Why? Reflections on the Loss of a Loved One_, writes that as a child he was imprisoned in a concentration camp where he lost his mother and infant brother. As an adult, he lost a child in a car accident. He wrote about his feelings of mourning and grief and came to the conclusion that a person "should always try to sing – even in sorrow." Rabbi Vorst says, "Death is an event which God does not leave to chance. Everything is planned by Him to the smallest detail. Such a drastic event as dying cannot be a matter of random chance." He talks about a "spiritual relationship – the spirit of the soul" and says: "Although the physical bond between parents and children can be broken (by death) their spiritual relationships cannot be. The soul or spirit of the departed person stays in contact with family members. The deceased knows what happens here. This is the idea that the soul lives on after death."

Reflections

One continues to see that those who lost a parent in early life often go on to follow in the lost parent's footsteps. If a father was a policeman or detective or lawyer, the son or daughter might become one also. If a father enjoyed food, his son or daughter might become a chef. If a mother or father had been generous, the adult child might be a big tipper and give to charity. If a parent suffered a particular disease, the offspring tend to go into medicine, research or another healing profession. Some become mental health practitioners and nurses. Many people say that carrying on the parent's career feels like a link to their parent – a completion of the parent's legacy.

A parent's words often carry too much power and off-hand comments can be hung onto and remembered as the truth. It is consoling to children who have lost a parent to know how much their parent loved them. The more they know, the more they could feel the love. Children also grow up wanting to know reasons to be proud of their parent. They want to know they were incredible people. They often sought specifics of who they were and what they accomplished – what made them special. Of equal importance, the children want to know that their parents had great memories of them – that they impacted their parent's life in a positive way. That brings them comfort.

CHAPTER 8
Ways People Heal

The "blankie" for the baby and toddler provides the illusion of the comforting parent and is experienced as a transitional object. Transitional objects help the child and later the adult by providing a way to maintain the union with the missing parent, often using these symbols during times of stress or fear. They are items that are familiar and comforting.

Sometimes the traits of the missing parent are projected onto God, who then becomes the transitional object and they merge into one. This familiarity becomes a source of comfort. Prayer is made to the parent/God and the identity of each becomes blurred. Yet, this has a way of providing renewed hope and faith, and assists in the ability to move forward in life. One can learn to see the parent in imagery. Imagery or a form of prayer or meditation are useful as ways to discuss unfinished business with the deceased parent or as a way to say goodbye. Imagery and meditation can facilitate healing.

A "clarity of life" is often acquired when a parent dies. It is a clearer way of looking at life, paying attention to where you are, where you are going and what is important to you. A sense of urgency occurs – a need to get where you are going as quickly as possible. It is the clear vision you would not have gotten to any other way or as quickly. People in time often learn how to live fully in each moment, make it count and feel a sense of confidence in a new way.

Many learn to put more emphasis on the value of people in their lives and on the enjoyment of interactions with loved ones. They learn to look at the big picture and not worry so much about details. They try to pass on to their family that life is precious. They encourage them to remember to see what is important in each moment – trying to make the ordinary extraordinary. Learning to savor the moments and enjoy the beauty of the sunsets, the changing seasons, the rare moments of true human communication, and not miss the pleasures in life is the goal.

The Younger Child and Healing

When a child is left with a surviving parent who is depressed, struggling with financial hardships and many life changes, the parent often becomes incapacitated, resulting in single parenting that is frequently inadequate parenting. The child often mirrors the parent's depression and incorporates this depressed affect, which hinders development and accomplishments. The loss of both parents then occurs when the surviving parent is incapacitated by loss of the spouse. The child feels alone, abandoned, and fearful of adding to the surviving parent's grief or being a burden.

It is important that the child be allowed to mourn the loss of the parent who actually died. In order to do this, one needs active support from the surviving parent. That parent needs to be able to tolerate his own as well as the child's pain. Mourning is a process, which allows the child to express grief. It is a psychological or emotional response to one's loss. It is an emotion that draws one toward the missing person. It arises from awareness of the discrepancy between the world that had been, is now, and that should have been. One wonders if the child has the capacity to mourn, but this is not really the problem. The issue is the absence of an empathic other person at a time of crucial need that constitutes the problem. The bereaved parent is often unable to provide the patience, affect, support and role-modeling the child needs to recover. The child then develops an inability to trust or to depend on the surviving adult. These children could develop a further lack of trust in themselves.

Grief is a natural emotion. It allows the trauma of loss, injury and deprivation to be expressed and dissipated in tears. It is a painful emotion, yet a necessary part that will lead to adjustment. Repressed grief can cause extensive damage physically and emotionally. In all emotions that are repressed – including grief – the energy content of the unexpressed emotion becomes stored and locked in the body. This tenses and injures the tissues and organs and distorts the flow of all other emotions. If a child hears "Don't cry," or "It's all right," or "It will be okay," he learns that tears and feelings are not acceptable and are wrong. However, if the child hears, "It's all right to cry, I know you're sad, go ahead, cry," the child is given clear permission to express what his reality is at that moment: sadness and loss. Each time a child is receiving acceptance and validation – he is learning to trust and respect his inner responses. He becomes more rooted in himself – from simple beginnings of being acknowledged and being allowed to express his emotions. This process plants the seeds of self-direction and gives way to inner authority, which springs forth and helps to make adult life a more joyful experience.

A loving adult who spends a lot of quality time with the child can do a great deal to promote healing. Many people describe their relationship with a grandmother, for example, as being the source of new traditions, warmth and positive memories that provided strength and a loving support system. Often a grandparent and other relatives of the deceased parent are able to help keep the parent alive for the child. They provide photographs and speak about the parent from various aspects of their lives. This often helps fill in the empty spaces and helps the child to answer questions about his own identity. Some tasks for the surviving parent include talking to the child, allowing him to ask questions, and reassuring the child he is still loved and safe and will be taken care of. The child needs to know he is not responsible for the loss. The use of rituals is also important for healing. It is very helpful if the parent allows himself to grieve and to have the child observe that. The child then learns to mirror the responses. It provides a road map for processing the feelings and being able to move forward. It is important to give the child explanations he can understand.

Those unable to trust report they were often not able to depend on the surviving parent. Their development is impeded, and they remain at the same developmental stage as they were at the time of the loss, or they progress slowly and in limited ways. Parental emotions and fears of being inadequate to the task at hand can be communicated overtly and covertly. With overreactions, the child responds and thinks simple things are dangerous. The child needs to learn a balanced perspective of reality that will sustain him toward adult independence. When the child expresses his emotions, regardless of the emotional content, the feelings need to be validated. It is usually dissipated in tears and followed by relief.

Often the child fears his parent's death was caused by his thoughts or naughty behavior. The child needs the surviving parent or other caretakers to appreciate the inner world of the child and to respond appropriately. He needs to be reassured it was not his fault or as a result of his thoughts or his behaviors. The child needs a role model for expression of his emotions. If the adult shows grief, the child will likewise express his feelings. He must know it is okay to cry. Tears are a tribute to the depth of true love. Having an adult who will show honesty is important. Children need reality, truth, sincerity. Any show of insincerity – even nonverbal cues will be confusing and will drain energy. It is important to answer the questions the child asks. The deceased parent's name should be used in conversation. Euphemisms such as "sleeping," "gone away," or "lost" should be avoided. This could confuse the child and cause fears of sleep, going away or getting lost. It also opens the door to fantasies that the parent will return, be found or wake up.

Many children have the fantasy that the parent still lives and can be found again. This can often be enacted in dreams even many years later. When the child retains the fantasy that the parent can be found again, this inhibits the potential for true replacement of the love object not just in childhood, but throughout life. Some children are able to maintain the image of the lost parent and accept another adult as a continuation or surrogate for the lost parent.

Children find ways to stay connected to their loved ones. This is how people naturally react to a death. Research has shown that up to two years later – and even longer – up to 74% of children said the parent was in heaven watching out for them – becoming their "guardian angel" – 43% still thought about the parent every day and 39% talked to the parent. They define grieving as "navigating transition from losing what you have to having what you've lost."

The child becomes healthy and adjusts best when the surviving or surrogate parent adjusts well to the crisis. This caring adult needs the ability to respond well to the child's emotions and needs as he goes through the normal childhood developmental stages. If this is not accomplished, the child has difficulty giving up the attachment to or investment in the lost parent. The capacity to mourn is important to adequate development. The developmental tasks are expected by one's culture to be mastered at a specific life stage. Failure to master these tasks leads to greater difficulty in the next developmental phase. Issues of bereavement are added onto the regular expected tasks. As one moves to the next phase, the developmental transitions could precipitate a resurgence of grief. Often a child has difficulty giving up the attachment to the lost parent and cannot integrate the reality in a healthier way. The search goes on forever for the parent whose death is denied and the person remains, to a significant degree, the child at that phase or age when the loss occurred.

When Nora was 10 years old, she had the opportunity to participate in group therapy after her father died. This helped her to know others had the same feelings as she did. She was, therefore, able to develop some stability and a sense of not being alone, and she felt more secure. Sometimes it is helpful for children to write the names of those who helped them during their period of mourning. All children fear they will lose someone else they love or that they themselves will die.

Tara, a 40-year-old woman who is a professional photographer, was 11 when she lost her father. She was told, "He went away." She was not taken to the funeral and never felt like she said "good-bye." She had no one with whom to share her pain. As an adult she believes this event had altered her life forever. Tara feels she was healed when she was able to make some peace for herself. She realized that even though their years together were too short, she had been able to give something to her father. What she gave him was "the invisible, pure joy a father gets from his child – the hugs, kisses, smiles and "I love you's." She knows in her heart that she brought him pleasure and enriched his life. She says he "lives on within her," and feels nurtured by his memory as she pursues her career. She believes that she chose photography because he gave her the gift of a camera.

Mourning the loss provides the ability to recall with affective re-experiencing, which leads to emotional distance from the trauma and gradually integrates the loss and helps reestablish equilibrium in everyday life. The child needs to re-experience the loss in each developmental stage as he grows and matures. The child has to lean more heavily on the surviving parent or other nurturing, caring, and reliable adult for the support necessary to face the loss, to grieve and to mourn. This will facilitate the development of skills needed to achieve success at each new stage of growth.

The parent or other care giving adult needs to be able to:

1. Utilize community resources for the child to receive whatever help is indicated, such as grief therapy.

2. Keep the family together.

3. Maintain the nature of the pre-loss relationships to each parent.

4. Give the child opportunity to express feelings, which will likely run the whole gamut of emotions, including confusion, anger and pain.

5. Help the child face the reality of the situation and foster the adjustment to the missing parent not being there in the natural environment.

6. Facilitate the adjustment and acceptance of the "new normal."

It has been observed that younger bereaved children had a higher incidence of behavioral problems. There were also higher exhibits of attention seeking among boys. Girls tended to be more withdrawn. Older boys tended toward more difficulty with concentration. There were a lot of depressive symptoms and guilt among the older children.

In latency, symbolism can be seen in the child's creativity, such as his or her artwork. A camp called "Comfort Zone Camp" in Richmond, Virginia was the source of healing for Cindy, a girl who lost her father at age 12. When Cindy was 18, she reported how this special camp helped her to grieve and to learn how to have fun again. She had felt she did not have the right to be happy ever again. She had felt she was alone in her experience, that no other child ever lost a parent. She could not confide in her friends nor talk to her mom. She kept everything inside. In the "Healing Circles," Cindy was able to talk about memories of her father, and others likewise shared their losses. She ultimately learned to cherish what she had through her memories, and to cherish what she currently had in her life. Cindy learned how to stay positive and stop dwelling on what is missing.

There are camps and programs all across the country that focus on children who have lost a parent. Many of these programs are at little or no cost. Their goals are to help the child learn how to cope with their new reality and begin to heal. Most importantly, they help the children to open up, express their emotions and realize they are not alone, that their grief is shared by many of their peers. It is crucial to learn they each have the right to be happy again.

Things a parent or other family member can do to help the child cope:

1) Do a lot of hugging – demonstrate that continuous love and affection will always be available.

2) Talk a lot (learn ways to express thoughts and feelings) to know there is no need for guilt or self-blame.

3) Seek out a bereavement support group, which is also helpful. It deals with the grief expression, fears, angers, sadness, guilt and acceptance. The typical support groups also have activities for the surviving parents and other caretakers. Both the children and adult groups meet simultaneously and then come together at the end for additional sharing.

4) Involvement in groups, individual or family therapy can help the child to use many forms of creativity such as presenting a token, a poem, song, or a picture symbolically to the deceased parent or to the surviving parent.

5) Talk within the family unit so the family is not driven apart.

The participation in groups or therapy helps people to feel less alone. They also help prepare the child for a return to school and facilitate the development of skills, which will enable the child to cope with the "new normal." It is important for the child to be able to recall the fun times together with the deceased parent, the places they went and the things they did. This helps the child reconnect with the lost parent and with their specialness with each other.

The Teenager and Healing

In the teen years, the struggle between autonomy and the need to be close, to be held, to be together, to be a part of, and to be secure is seen. There is often anger at injustice in the world and, on a personal level, anger at the surviving parent as well as at the deceased parent. There is often an increase in fear and anxiety. In this group, the symptoms seen often were depression, feelings of abandonment, hopelessness, anxiety, greater sensitivity to stress and heightened dependency needs. These feelings waxed and waned over time. Healing can be realized when there is a resolution of ambivalence and guilt.

Some teens become "parentified" when a parent dies. They "become the parent" by identifying with the parent. This role is often inadvertently assigned to the child by the surviving parent who has placed unreasonable expectations on the child. The roles placed onto them are too burdensome. The parentified child is faced with too large a job and he cannot do it all. He feels it is his job to care for the remaining parent and ends up feeling lost, insecure and unsafe.

Sadie, a 28-year-old woman who lost her mother when she was 14, became overburdened by expectations placed on her. She had to care for the family and for her father. The family also had to move to another home in a new neighborhood, which meant her life changed abruptly in every aspect. Her adjustment to her new school was difficult. She was unable to finish her homework and began to think of herself as "a person who doesn't finish things." This belief about herself continued. Sadie dropped out of school, has had several jobs and many short-term relationships. After being in therapy, she was able to revisit her past and began to heal. Sadie is now beginning to move from never finishing anything to one who is able to set realistic goals and complete tasks. She is finally healing her wounds.

When Tony, a 25 year old man, looked back on his early teen years, he realized his maternal grandmother helped him to heal. When his mother died, he spent a lot of time with his grandmother who told him stories of happy times he and his mother shared when he was a young child. Tony's grandmother shared happy times from his mother's life with him. He took great comfort in hearing how happy he always made his mother and also in hearing how much his mother loved him. His grandmother assured him that his mother would have been so proud of him and his accomplishments in school. Tony and his grandmother were a mutual support system for each other. If a child receives love, respect and compassion, he is given an extraordinary healing gift.

Knowing our deceased parent provided unconditional love goes a long way toward bringing about healing. Mark, a successful 30-year-old man, lost his father at age 15. He shared the secret of his success. Before his heart surgery, his father gave him a note in case he did not survive his surgery, which unfortunately he did not. The note became this young man's treasure. It contained the loving words he most needed to hear in order to live a productive life. His father's note expressed his pride in his son's intelligence and scholastic accomplishments. He wrote that Mark had great gifts that must be cherished. As Mark grew to manhood, he felt his father was always at his side, cheering him on. When facing challenges, he was always sure he would succeed and he believes he will continue to be a success in his chosen field.

Melanie, a 17-year-old young woman, was 14 when she lost her uncle, who was her best friend. Melanie wrote an essay about the loss she felt when he died and how she was able to cope. Excerpts of this essay are reprinted here. "When I looked into his twinkling kind blue eyes, I always knew I was safe and loved." She describes how he waited for her each day after school at her bus stop. He was her after-school caretaker/ playmate. After a long time of grief and mourning, she came to realize how lucky she was to have this man in her life.

Melanie learned about his death when she was away at summer camp. She says she "cried millions and millions of tears." It was raining very hard when her mother came to get her from camp. Her mother explained, "It is raining because all the angels are crying because they know your beloved uncle was taken away from you." Melanie says that after his death and for a long time, she felt very angry at him. She felt he lied to her and did not keep his promise to "be there always." Melanie later realized he had left her with some tangible material mementos and also with the gift of love few people ever felt. Years later, she describes his love as total, abundant and unconditional. Melanie reports that he was her mentor, protector, source of advice and guidance, and he helped her to get through rough times. Melanie believes his love has contributed in a very positive way to who she is today.

One of the tasks of working through the grief process includes making the transition to future life. To do this one must acknowledge the reality of the loss. Going to the funeral, talking to people, experiencing the pain and sharing feelings are some of the steps to take. One must adjust to the new environment, finding ways to remember the person, which helps one to reinvest emotional energy and be able to move forward, finding renewed control of one's life. Some people find it helpful to keep a journal as they return to daily living. It typically takes from 18 to 24 months to stabilize after a loss. When one finds ways to remember and memorialize a parent, energies are reinvested, and feelings will be less severe each time they recur.

In death, the deceased person takes on so much power. We seek the approval of our mother or father – but in fact – we rarely have an accurate vision of what kind of life our parent would have approved. When our parent goes away too soon, a piece of our past and a piece of our future is taken as well. The question one often ponders is: If my mother or my father had lived, how would my life have been different? One often believes: If my mother or my father had lived, this or that would have happened differently, or would not have happened and I would have been _____. (Fill in the blank)

Ask yourself – what are the threads that continue in your life? What connects you to your parents? What continues to influence you from the knowledge of the person your parent or parents were? What are the positive influences that still resonate in your life? Have there been any positive influences, any good that has come to you through the years? Has your loss influenced your way of life, your values, your core beliefs, your career path or other life choices? Answering these questions will help one to explore inward and hopefully empower one to live a more fulfilled life. Much creativity comes from deep within, from inner pain and sadness. Our creative works come from this secret place and often bring about healing.

The death of a parent at a young age affects later life: For example, a person who creates works of art or literature or music as ways to express emotions can reach greater creative depths that might never have been reached otherwise. Some inspiration comes through dreams. The expression creates a new healing on both an emotional and physical level. We have all been given gifts by our parents and usually it is the parent we lost as a youngster or young adult who gives us our most valued gifts. These are the gifts that guide us through our lives, help form us, and often lead us to our careers. It is frequently because of who these people were and their inspiration and impact on us that we become who we become. If we can heal our wounds, we are able to realize our best selves through these gifts.

The ideal goal is for the child and teenager to become able to identify with goals and interests of their lost parent, using this focus as the departure point for future life work. He might become a teacher or a businessman or a lawyer, etc., following in his parent's footprints. Often a person goes into the medical field or research to find a cure for his parent's illness. Sometimes choosing hobbies that were part of the parent's life are a way to hold the parent within the self.

Angela, a 45-year-old woman, lost her mother at 15 and became a film director. She says that, "Many films bring back the painful experience of my mother's death, especially films that address the mother/daughter relationship or a mother's illness." Angela sees her work as a way to confront her demons. The films are "images that tell the story, making my inner work meaningful. They help express struggles, pains and emotions." Angela feels the loss of her mother as a loss of a part of herself. She yearns for her mother and never completely separates from her. In her work, Angela tries to retrieve her lost mother, and in some real life instances, becomes like her mother in her behavior and attitude. In many work situations, Angela often takes on a lot of the responsibilities and becomes like a mother in the work place.

Tania, a young woman of 30, lost her father at age 12. She finally went into therapy to mourn her loss as an adult. She then realized her father had been an artist. Tania began to recall her father's love of beauty and nature and she began to look forward to becoming an artist also. As an adult, Tania went to art school and developed her own style of creativity. She says she is very happy in her new career as an artist.

Connie, a 35 year old woman, was 15 when her father suffered a heart attack at age 53. She claims it had taken her until adulthood to be able to say, "My father is dead." With therapy, she finally was able to focus on creating her own healthier lifestyle. She strives to "live long enough to see my children grow up and become a grandmother." Connie went to college as an adult and became a cardiac nurse because of her father's illness.

Vicki, a 40-year-old woman, was 17 when she lost her father as a result of violence. She was then determined to become a lawyer. Today, the focus of her work is to put an end to violence. Vicki is very involved in activities that bring about violence awareness. She reports that as a younger woman, she had a problem trusting others, even when someone was being kind to her. Vicki had received grief counseling in her 20s, which helped her to learn how to relax, accept pleasure, and be able to trust again. Vicki was able to marry a man who is emotionally supportive, sensitive and caring. This provides her with the right balance between her home life and the often stressful work she has chosen.

Bill, a man in his 40s, was 15 when he lost his father, who was very interested in music. He immediately followed his father's love for music. After his father's death, while still in high school, Bill played in a band and later became a music teacher. He realized he was having trouble forming close relationships with women when he was in his 20s. After receiving counseling, he was then able to marry and takes a lot of pride in being a good father and caring husband. He works hard, yet spends a lot of time with his wife and children. Bill has achieved his goal to make up for all he missed in childhood and to "live my life to the fullest."

Wendy, a young woman, became a psychologist and works with people who have religious issues. She teaches them to get in touch with their own beliefs. She was deprived of participation in religious services at her home following the death of her mother when she was 14. As a result, it took her years to be able to "tolerate any religious practices." Her interest in her professional choice grew as she received counseling and realized how strong her bond was to her mother, which was passed along to her without words. Wendy continues to feel a strong connection with her mother's spirit.

One often becomes a doctor, lawyer, nurse, medical researcher, writer, poet, world traveler, businessperson, architect, florist, etc. as a result of the relationship with the deceased parent. The loss of a parent to a particular illness might lead the young adult to take on missions to find a cure or fight the disease. They wish to turn grief and loss into something positive and beneficial in the parent's honor or to carry on their legacy.

The Young Adult and Healing

The adult who did not mourn adequately often remains immature and could exhibit character deficits. Grief is incorporated into the child's future adult personality as the death of his parent shapes his entire lifetime. Many children grew up with a widowed parent who was too often overly protective, fearful for the child's safety and fearful for his own health, who worried especially about "who will care for my children if something happens to me?"

Those who become stuck in childhood conditioning and negative environments carry excess baggage into adulthood where they tend to create and recreate the same scenarios. One often continues to exhibit feelings of inadequacy, a lack of self-love, damaged self-esteem, devaluation of his parent or himself, decreased need fulfillment, and inability to trust. The child may have known about his surviving parent's pain on an intuitive level and, having strong empathy, might feel guilty when he focuses on himself. The stages of grief one needs to go through at any age are denial, anger, bargaining, depression and eventually acceptance. These stages can be completed at the time of the loss or can take many years and often get completed in adulthood. Rage and other hidden emotions can get expressed through the body throughout life. These can include headaches, backaches, depression, sexual problems or compulsive behaviors. When those who use denial or repression as defense mechanisms are able to learn to acknowledge and express loss and grief feelings, their depression is usually lifted and relief is felt.

One technique that can be used in therapy is to go back and revisit the "Child" of your past in order to re-experience the emotions until they become less intense. Some clients report that their feelings then become less frightening and they feel safer. They are no longer afraid of those parts of themselves. Some ways to do this exercise is through the recording of dreams, creating art, writing poetry, keeping a journal, doing dance or music therapy and practicing visualization. Telling our stories is vital and has been very healing to many people. These techniques may enable an incorporation of the loss and promote recovery. Making a toast to the deceased at holiday gatherings, writing a letter to the loved one, looking at photographs and sharing memories will also aid in recovery.

It is helpful for an adult to talk about his or her childhood losses. This helps to change the perspective from that of a child to that of an adult who has developed some insight to both himself and to his parent as an individual. As an adult, one of the healing techniques used is to have the person stand in the parent's shoes to see who the parent was, to see the beliefs, the life, the strengths, the failings and the various roles the parent played in his own life. Working on unfinished business, working on the "inner parent" by doing dream work and journal writing can also help. Many people also heal by being in therapy, which helps to provide a clear vision of the whole family system. One can then see old patterns with more clarity. One learns to see ways the family members had been enmeshed or estranged. It is like a veil lifting. Healing can come by working on the self within the family dynamics from the past as well as on current life relationships. Ideally, new dynamics with siblings and closer family bonds can be formed.

The family system and family dynamics is often thrown into chaos. With new clarity of vision one can see unfinished business and issues never before realized. One can see secrets, denials and old relationship issues which might be carried into present day life. There could be revivals of old jealousies or a renewal of commitment to the importance of family. When one has dreams of the parent and the past, the psyche is trying to reveal information. It becomes clear that although the parent is gone, something else is living on. The deceased do live through us in many ways. Looking within at the child part of oneself, one can see what that part of the self still needs. One can find the nurturing part of the parent inside and learn how to let that part grow. One then can learn to become one's own "good and nurturing parent." The goal is to look at one's life and pay attention to where one is going and what is important.

A troubling milestone is often expressed when a son or daughter has lived longer than the parent did. Though difficult to process, dealing with long buried emotions can be a useful growth experience. If one is holding onto beliefs about the parents' expectations and disappointments, these need to be worked through in therapy, and the goal is to be able to release these beliefs since they are usually found to be counterproductive. One can learn to rebuild and find satisfying relationships with others in love and work. Eventually, one can reach peace, love and acceptance. It helps to be able to reach the point where one can focus on the positive memories. It helps if one can reflect on what one honors and admires in the parent and make it part of oneself. Realizing who their parents were helped a lot of people to get on with their own achievements and to realize their own potential, their own needs and their personal goals and dreams. Successfully surpassing the level their deceased parents were at educationally, financially or personally is something people often need to be taught and encouraged to do.

Through therapy a lot of people have learned some important coping skills such as relaxation and stress-reduction techniques. They have learned how to help care for themselves better, how to relieve anxiety and fears and how to become their own "good parent." Many people report that they were able to regain their own sense of a stronger self and learn to be more self-reliant and independent. They had to learn that they would be able to take care of themselves and/or their children no matter what happened in their lives. They also had to learn to take good care of themselves physically so fears of illness could be kept under control.

Another healing technique is making a living memory-connection, such as researching the deceased's life through letters, journals and conversations with family and friends. One can write letters to the deceased and write one back as if it were from the deceased. One can also write a biography of the deceased parent or of the family. Surrounding oneself with compassionate and empathetic people is also healing while one is going through this process.

Grief is an active process. It is not something that happens to you, but rather something that must be experienced. A sense of being helpless to prevent the loss of a loved one may lull some into thinking that there is nothing that can be done about grief. In actuality, there are four stages of grief that ideally will be experienced according to each individual timetable:

1) Accepting the reality of the loss.

2) Experiencing the pain.

3) Adjusting to the new environment.

4) Re-investing the emotional energy.

One of the aspects experienced with loss that is very difficult to handle is the sadness and regret when one could not tell a parent "goodbye," could not attend the funeral or could not go to the cemetery. Visiting the cemetery and spending time at a parent's grave can be a healing experience. Knowing that their family is actually there behind the tombstone often provides solemnity and a peaceful feeling of knowing they are close by. Some comfort themselves with the belief the deceased will be seen again at their own death. Rituals are usually ways to bring about healing. Going to the cemetery, visiting graves of loved ones and following the rituals that are usually part of every culture's funeral services can help one to heal. They mark the loss of a member of that culture or of a certain faith. These rituals sanction the expression of grief and allow the mourners to go on with their lives. It is important for the mourners to use special rituals that address individual belief systems and personal needs.

Prayer and religious ritual are also important for the ongoing healing of the individual. In Judaism, for example, the holiday of Yom Kippur, the Day of Atonement, has a special service called Yiskor, which includes prayers to pay respect to and allow for remembrance of all those we have lost. This is one of the special prayers that might be recited: "On this Day of Atonement we recall with gratitude our loved ones whose days on earth were a blessing and whose memory abides as a source of consolation and inspiration. Enriched by their example, guided by their teaching, ennobled by their love we walk the road of life. Thus, in word and in deed do we honor their memory and render them our tribute of love."

A special way to honor a deceased loved one is to pass on that person's name to a new baby such as a child or grandchild. There is a sense of immortality when the new life carries on the name. The deceased lives on through their loved ones who carry on their good name, good deeds, physical, or emotional characteristics. The descendants learn about those whose names they carry through family stories, photographs and other mementos. They often feel the deceased parent's soul gets passed on to live again in the newborn life.

Since emotions get reactivated at anniversary times, it is healing when people are able to talk about their feelings. Visiting the gravesite, attending a religious service, lighting a candle and focusing on the parent in health and strength can also be healing. Some people feel sadness and loneliness and a strong missing of the parent at anniversary times. They focus on the loss, especially at holiday and milestone events. Many women and men spoke about observing religious rituals and feeling "like my mother" or "like my father" in those moments. They take pride in passing on the parents' rituals in the form of religion, education, kindness, charity and other forms of giving. Some take pride in passing on the parent's good values. Others adopt the parent's hobbies, such as love of flowers, gardening, reading, cooking, creativity in music, art, writing, poetry, film, design, etc. Others go into the same career as the parents.

Another way to honor a dearly loved person is to use the things (clothing, household items, china, silver, jewelry) that are left. There are meaningful mementos left that carry the essence of the departed and bring good memories and love and remembered feelings of closeness. One often feels as though our parent is smiling down at us when we wear or use one of their precious possessions or cook their favorite foods.

Many self-help or healing organizations have been founded by people who have lost parents. Their goals are to help others who experience loss of self-esteem, who have an inability to function or flourish at their optimal level, or who might need material resources or mentoring or someone to talk to in order to move on in their life with less stress and the knowledge they are not alone. When one experiences anger at the deceased parent that cannot abate, it is often important and helpful to focus on their need to forgive the parent for leaving too soon. One needs to face the role that anger plays. Some say, "If I give up my anger, who am I?" With the healing of anger comes the lessening of being an anxious, sad or phobic person. Forgiveness helps to soften the person's affect, and there is less emotion in expressed feelings. It enables a letting go of blocked energy. One can then have more fullness in life, and allow other feelings to prevail. People report that they heal more quickly when they allow themselves a time to be with their grief fully and then the time to let go gradually occurs.

Prior to my own grief work, anger at my father included anger for: being ill, dying too young, leaving us when we were all still so needy of him, working such long hours, allowing mom to be so anxious and fearful, not asserting his own needs, not spending more time with me alone and with us all as a family, not seeing me get married, not walking me down the aisle, not seeing me as a mother, not being there to enjoy my children (who would have been the three most precious parts of his life), not being there for my children to know, love, enjoy and learn from.

In addition to psychotherapy and grief work, some other healing processes have been helpful. These include: visualization, meditation, relaxation skills, massage and other types of bodywork therapy, and journal writing. Writing one's own story is very beneficial to people who enjoy writing. Each time you write and rewrite the same story, the event and the memory become more clearly defined. One keeps getting more, different and deeper experiences, memories, feelings and eventually healing. It is important to keep one's own story and one's ancestral stories alive. Forgiveness exercises are also useful. Some questions asked are "What do I have trouble forgiving my parent for?" Or "I'm still angry at my parent for..." This is an important part of anger work which helps lead to healing.

Terry, a 40-year-old woman, felt she had a lot of anger when she lost her father as a teenager. Through grief work, she says she had connected with her father's character. She realized that from him, she learned to be affectionate, strong, wise and independent. When feeling sad or lonely, she wrote poetry as her father had done. She was eventually able to let go of her anger. Terry's greatest pleasure came when her own child was born. She saw her father in her son and felt she had her father back. Terry feels his essence lives on through her child. She believes her driving force through her life has been her father. When she sees how well she is doing, she thinks: "OK, Daddy, we made it."

For many women who grew up and married in the 1950s and 1960s, there was the belief that one got married and lived happily ever after. For those who lost their fathers as teens, the rush to marriage, usually at a young age, was a push toward seeking safety and security and also replacing their lost father. As part of this group, I literally never thought one day beyond my wedding.

Some of these women had an idealized, perfect father image that negatively affects their current relationships with husbands or children. Healing can be brought about if they explore their relationship with their fathers. If there is not much known about the person he was, they should learn as much as possible about him from his family and friends. A lot can be learned by reading old letters, looking at family photos and exploring his positive and negative aspects. As more information becomes known, he begins to feel more like a real person. These women can then begin to make attempts toward closeness with the real men in their life. They will then be more able to learn about themselves and how they participated in battles and estrangements and relationship issues. Hopefully, they can eventually move on toward a more satisfying life.

Molly, a 50-year-old woman, described losing her 22-year-old father in the Vietnam War when she was a young child. All she knew about him was that he was a musician and played guitar. After years of searching for him, waiting for him to return and fantasizing what her life might/should have been, she sought help. Eventually, she was able to marry and had a son. She learned how to celebrate her father's gifts. Molly realized her son had musical talent and gave her father's guitar to him. She is filled with joy to know that she and her son help keep her father's memory alive through music. Molly also learned that her father had a wonderful sense of humor, which she shares. She allows herself to feel happy and is able to use humor to make herself and others laugh. Laughter is a positive road to healthy healing.

Nancy, a 35-year-old woman, talked about keeping a journal when she became pregnant with her first child. Years later, she read her journal and was surprised to see that she began her first sentence with "My mother died when I was 12." As a way to deal with her loss, Nancy has learned to incorporate thoughts of "what would my mom do in this situation?" This helps her to make positive choices in her life. She knows she will never see her mom grow old. She only has an image of her as a very young woman. Nancy has no role model for growing older and feels each day is an adventure into uncharted territory, yet she feels confident that she will be alright. Learning more about her mother helped her to know herself better, and she has learned to trust herself.

If one is lucky enough to lose a parent at an older age, one is able to observe how the parent dealt with the dying process and how the parent felt about his/her life and death. This has a profound impact, and one often gets to observe that at life's end, work ceases to matter. All that matters and all that's left at the end is love and relationships. When we see that, it impacts us greatly. It is a powerful lesson one does not easily forget and can be practiced as a model for living a richer life. Knowing one's parent is ill and dying, one is hopefully able to spend some quality time. Those able to have that meaningful time together were able to express love for each other and were able to say "goodbye." People say that precious time together helped them to get through the pain and sadness more easily.

The impact of the death of a parent affects all aspects of one's life. In one's adult years, all aspects of life come into question. One re-examines career, relationships, marriage, spirituality, values, etc. One tends to re-evaluate what is of most importance and redirect life with new priorities. When the death of a parent comes in adulthood, the impact of the death on a marriage can cause stress. While a person grieves, much emotion comes to the surface and the partner can become overwhelmed and unable to be there emotionally. There is often a new clarity of vision that comes to shed light on the marriage system when the grieving person sees his or her needs are not being met. There could be a new awareness of what was holding the marriage together, what might not be working any more and perhaps with the help of marital or family therapy, there will be a new direction toward healing the marriage.

A positive aspect of healing can come from the creation of memorials from the heart. This is a way to remember and honor their legacies. One can remember those who touched our lives by giving back to others we love or to the community. It is a mitzvah (or good deed) to create a meaningful legacy as a way to remember and honor our loved ones.

Just like in post-traumatic stress disorder, there will always be memories or flashbacks to events or feelings that present out of the blue. This usually occurs after a "trigger button" is pushed. The memory or the feeling presents as if it is a new body feeling or emotional reaction. The body never forgets – the body memory is always there. Creating an alliance or healthy attachment to a caregiver, therapist or other competent adult is very important. One needs to feel safe in both the external and internal world. Creating a "holding environment" is important to the person in pain.

Healing goals include: (1) being able to cope with a more balanced internal environment, with the reactions becoming more mild and less sudden or less intense; (2) increasing the ability to maintain connections with others; (3) improving one's ability to soothe or comfort oneself; (4) securing and maintaining a positive self-identity; (5) learning to gain control over one's current life; (6) finding a safe base through the ability to trust and acquire and maintain secure attachments.

Reflections

The child at every stage of development needs to feel permitted to express emotions of anger, fear, hate, grief, etc. If these emotions are judged as negative or unacceptable, the child blocks them off or represses them. The child then becomes depressed and might tend to develop a negative attitude toward daily life or feel more hopeless about the future. He could become stuck in an endless search for a lost idyllic relationship. The child who is allowed and encouraged to express emotions learns feelings are valid and that he or she has the power and the right to express them. Thus begins the healing process.

There are some children who are more resilient. Maybe it is good genes or perhaps something good or positive happened in early childhood. A child who initially bonded well may have an easier time making an adjustment. It all depends on the way things are handled. The emotional adjustment of significant adults around the child will reduce the likelihood of future emotional difficulties. The child needs a consistent, predictable relationship with at least one caring adult. Compassion for the person in mourning is essential. It diminishes the sense of alienation.

There are many people who are less vulnerable to intense emotional pain, who are relatively free of fear and guilt and have a more positive life energy. They will have more ability to bounce back after a loss, and will not become totally devastated. They will be more honest and direct when expressing their emotions. The person who has the most emotional strength will exhibit the least amount of physical illness and will remain healthy intellectually as well. These people will be the most able to respond to life challenges in a healthy and positive way.

Even though anniversary reactions persist and are a part of the mourning process that continues over the years, the intensity of the memories and emotions often becomes less over time. The duration of the reactions is also less intense. One then has the energy to reinvest in the process of life and living. Even as one moves forward and heals to the best of one's ability, one will always remember one's parents, remain connected to them on a visceral level, and will always believe it was too soon to say "goodbye."

REFERENCES & RESOURCES

Akhtar, Salman, *Matters of Life and Death*, Karnac Books, 2010.

Album, Mitch, *Tuesdays with Morrie*, Doubleday, 1997.

The American Academy of Bereavement, 1-800-726-3888.

Altschul, Sol (ed.), *Childhood Bereavement and Its Aftermath*. International Universities Press, Inc., 1993.

The Barr-Harris Center, Chicago, IL.

Brodsky, Harold, *First Love and Other Sorrows*, Holt Paperbacks, 1998.

Brown, Les, *Live Your Dreams*, William-Morrow & Co., 1993.

Crystal, Billy, *700 Sundays*, Warner Books, 2005.

Dayan, Yael, *My Father/His Daughter*, Farrar Straus & Giroux, 1985.

Edelman, Hope, *Motherless Daughters*, DaCapo Press, 1994.

Eisenstadt, Marvin, André Haynal, Pierre Rentchnick, and Pierre de Senarclens, *Parental Loss and Achievement*, International Universities Press, 1989.

Feldman, Gayle, *You Don't Have to Be Your Mother*, W. W. Norton & Co., Inc., 1994.

Fischer, H. Keith, M.D., M.Sc. and Barney M. Olin, M.D., M.Sc. *"Psychogenic Determination of Time of Illness or Death by Anniversary Reactions and Emotional Deadlines,"* June 1972 – 18th Annual Meeting, Academy of Psychosomatic Medicine, Sarasota, Florida.

Gordon, Mary, *The Shadow Man*, Random House, 1996.

Greenspun, Adele Aron, *Daddies*, Philomel Books, New York, 1991.

Hilgard, Josephine, *"Reenactments of Anniversary Times."* Psychiatry, Volume 16, 1953.

Horn, Dara, *In the Image*, W. W. Norton & Co., Inc., 2002.

Institute for Psychoanalysis, 180 N. Michigan Avenue, Chicago, IL 60601, 312-726-6300.

Journal of Humanistic Education and Development, Volume 30, March 1992.

Kellerman, Jonathan, *Dr. Death*, Ballantine Books, 2000.

Kellerman, Jonathan, *Time Bomb,* Ballantine Books, 1990.

Kennedy, Alexandra, *Passage to a New Way of Living,* Harper Collins, 1991.

King, Bernice, *Hard Questions, Heart Answers,* Three Rivers Press, 1997.

"Parameters of Grief–Research of Bereavement," The National Psychologist, July-August 1998.

Pittman, Frank, *"The Masculine Mystique,"* The Networker, May/June 1990.

Shane, Estelle and Morton, *Object Loss and Self-Object Loss: "A Consideration of Self Psychology's Contribution to Understanding Mourning and the Failure to Mourn,"* The Annual of Psychoanalysis, Volume 18, 1990.

Tan, Amy, Interview in Philadelphia Inquirer, Magazine section, February 2001.

Thomas, Dylan, *Collected Poems,* New Directions, 2010.

Viorst, Judith, *Necessary Losses,* Simon and Schuster, 1986.